SMIKE

From the BBC television production of Smike

Exclusive distributors:
Music Sales Limited
78 Newman Street
London W1P 3LA
Music Sales PTY Limited
27 Clarendon Street
Artarmon, Sydney
Australia 2064.

SMIKE

A POP MUSICAL FREELY BASED ON CHARLES DICKENS' NICHOLAS NICKLEBY.

WRITTEN BY ROGER HOLMAN & SIMON MAY.

BASED ON AN ORIGINAL PRODUCTION BY THE BOYS OF KINGSTON GRAMMAR SCHOOL (LIBRETTO WRITTEN BY ROGER HOLMAN, SIMON MAY AND CLIVE BARNETT).

PREFACE

Since the first performance of SMIKE in 1973, SMIKE has been adapted for BBC Television by Paul Ciani and John Morley, revised and added to for different versions in the U.K., South Africa and Eire, by Peter Coe (director of the original production of OLIVER), Pinetown Junior School (Durban), Ken Linge, Bill Cadman, the boys of Christian Brothers, Synge Street (Dublin) and Holmewood House School (Tunbridge Wells). These are only some of those who have involved themselves with SMIKE, and to all those others not mentioned please accept our apologies.

It has been interesting to see that every production has been completely different, and so even now the present libretto is by no means definitive. The songs and libretto are now available for any school or amateur dramatic society to use to meet the requirements of their own production. Many variations are possible. For example the inclusion of girls in both the 19th and 20th Century sequences is possible. Some schools may wish to exclude the Saracens Head Scene (Act 1 scene 2) and go straight from the 20th Century classroom to Dotheboys Hall. Not all the scene changes may be possible, and for the Dotheboys Hall scenes an ingenious designer may well decide to incorporate the Squeers parlour room and the boys' quarters into one composite set. It is our view that the only requirement for a successful production of SMIKE is an open mind, a sense of fun, a love of Dickens and music, and plenty of energy!

The music to SMIKE is available from Music Sales Ltd., 78 Newman Street, London W.1.

An LP of the BBC TV version of SMIKE is available on Pye Records (NSPL 18423) We would be grateful if producers would include this information on their programme notes!

CHARACTERS

SMEETON . . . . SMIKE

NICHOLLS . . . . NICHOLAS NICKLEBY

HEADMASTER . . . . MR. SQUEERS

MRS. SQUEERS

MISS GRANT . . . . MISS FANNY SQUEERS

TUBBY - a bully . . . . WACKFORD SQUEERS JNR.

BROWN - a wag . . . . BOLDER

COATES - a grumbler . . . . COBBEY

MARSH . . . . GRAYMARSH

PLANK - a slow boy. . . . . MASTER BELLING

MR. RALPH NICKLEBY

MR. SNAWLEY

RICHARD - Landlord of the Saracen's Head

TILDA - friend of Miss Fanny Squeers

BOYS

ACT ONE

Scene 1   Modern School

              Transition

Scene 2   The Saracen's Head

Scene 3   Outside Dotheboys Hall

Scene 4   The Squeers' Parlour.   Dotheboys Hall

Scene 5   Schoolroom.   Dotheboys Hall

Scene 6   The Squeers' Parlour.   Dotheboys Hall

Interval

ACT TWO

Scene 1   Classroom.   Dotheboys Hall

              Transition

Scene 2   Modern School

MUSIC

ACT ONE

1. OVERTURE (GOING TO SCHOOL)

    into

    DAILY CHANT (4 bars intro)

2. DOING THINGS BY NUMBERS

3. HERE I AM

4. STOP AND JUST THINK WHO YOU COULD BE

5. TRANSITION MUSIC

6. YOUNGSTERS' INTERESTS AT HEART

7. WACKFORD, FANNY, SQUEERSY & ME

8. DOTHEBOYS HALL

9. DOING THINGS BY NUMBERS (REPRISE)

10. BETTER OFF THE WAY I AM

11. DON'T LET LIFE GET YOU DOWN

EDITOR'S NOTE:

*THE TECHNIQUE OF SLIDE SCREENS COULD BE
SIMPLIFIED BY USING A SINGLE SCREEN WITH
SLIDE PROJECTOR OR EVEN BE REPLACED BY
ANY OTHER SUITABLE METHOD WHICH THE
DIRECTOR FEELS WOULD PRESENT SMEETON'S
BACKGROUND*

ACT ONE

Scene One

OVERTURE

During the slow section of the music the HOUSE LIGHTS dim and the tabs are raised slowly. SMEETON is discovered alone amid a classroom of empty desks. He is sitting quite still. We cannot see his face. The lights are low.

Above the desks, at varying heights and depths, are hung four SLIDE SCREENS all of different sizes (from about 4' x 4' to as much as 9' x 6'). At this point they all show blackboards with different scripts connected with school life (e.g. Latin verbs, mathematical formulae etc.)

As the Overture progresses into the "SMIKE" Theme SMEETON looks up and stares blankly towards the audience.

A fast moving and emotive sequence using "multi-screen" fade/dissolve techniques begins on the screens. The purpose of this sequence is to show something of SMEETON'S background: e.g. as a baby in a pram, as a three year old playing with his parents, a car crash, being held by relatives at a funeral, as well as various attitudes of him alone during a parentless childhood.

During the "BELIEVE" theme all the screens return to the one slide depicting the car crash. They hold on this slide until "BRIMSTONE AND TREACLE" music.

As the "BRIMSTONE AND TREACLE" music begins the SCREENS are flown out, and the BOYS file into the classroom in a simple dance/movement routine. SMEETON remains motionless at his desk.

On the drum beats leading into the "DAILY TEST" HEADMASTER makes his entrance. He is a large, rather degenerate looking man. His entrance is pompous and flamboyant.

MISS GRANT enters from the opposite side of stage, and stands over the boys as they prepare for the Test. She looks old for her thirty years and is dressed accordingly in a tweed suit and horn rimmed spectacles.

DAILY CHANT SONG

Elaborate and regimented musical ritual. In Unison, the class bring out pens, paper and their comments on the Test are counterposed to the questions asked by the HEADMASTER.

The routine is designed so that the pupils finish by presenting their papers to MISS GRANT.

During the Test the HEADMASTER delivers the questions in an impersonal way. He faces the audience and almost seems to ignore the children. He is lost in a kind of reverie, only aware of his self-importance.

"DAILY TEST CHANT"

4 bars Intro.

HEADMASTER: WHAT WAS THE DATE OF GLADSTONE'S BAG?
CLASS: THE DAILY TEST IS SUCH A DRAG

HEADMASTER: WHO INVENTED ELECTRIC SPARKS?
CLASS: EVERYONE HAS TO GET FULL MARKS

HEADMASTER: HOW HIGH CAN A KANGAROO BOUNCE?
CLASS: THE DAILY TEST IS ALL THAT COUNTS

HEADMASTER: HOW LONG WAS QUEEN VICTORIA'S BEARD?
CLASS: THE TEST IS WHAT WE'VE ALWAYS FEARED

HEADMASTER: WHY DOES GRAVITY MAKE THINGS DROP?
CLASS: HE ONLY LIKES KIDS WHO COME TOP

HEADMASTER: WHEN WAS MAGNA CARTA SIGNED?
CLASS: OVER THE YEARS WE'VE BECOME RESIGNED

HEADMASTER: WHAT IS THE RAINFALL IN PERU?
CLASS: IT'S SUCH A USELESS THING TO DO

HEADMASTER: WHICH IS LIGHTER, GAS OR AIR?
CLASS: WE DON'T KNOW AND WE DON'T CARE

HEADMASTER: WHAT COUNTRY DID COLUMBUS FIND?
CLASS: THE DAILY TEST IS SUCH A BIND

HEADMASTER: TOWARDS WHAT SEA DOES THE HUMBER FLOW?
CLASS: DO WE REALLY NEED TO KNOW

HEADMASTER: WHAT WAS THE DATE OF AGINCOURT?
CLASS: I THINK HE ASKED US THAT BEFORE

HEADMASTER: HOW MANY INCHES IN A MILE?
CLASS: THE DAILY TEST IS SUCH A TRIAL

HEADMASTER: THE DATE OF THE TREATY OF AMSTERDAM?
CLASS: WE DON'T REALLY GIVE A DAMN

HEADMASTER: WHY IS THE BRITISH EMPIRE BEST?
CLASS: ONE DAY WE'LL STOP HIS CRUMMY TEST

Straight into next song: DOING THINGS BY NUMBERS
(During this number, lighting fades on HEADMASTER and MISS GRANT
who are some distance away from the boys).

Song: "DOING THINGS BY NUMBERS"

Chorus:
ALL OF OUR LIFE IS SPENT
DOING THINGS BY NUMBERS
DO THAT! DO THIS! NO, DON'T DO THAT!
BUT DO EVERYTHING I SAY,
DO EVERYTHING I SAY.

Verse 1:
JOIN THE QUEUE
AND WAIT TILL THEY CALL YOUR NUMBER
HOW D'YOU DO?
TELL ME YOUR NUMBER AND NAME.
WE'RE LIVING IN THE KIND OF WORLD WHERE IT
PAYS TO BE OLD.
WE'RE PUSHED AROUND, AND JUST LIKE CLOWNS
WE DO WHAT WE'RE TOLD

Chorus: a)
ONE, TWO BUCKLE MY SHOE
THREE, FOUR SHUT THAT DOOR
FIVE, SIX, SEVEN, EIGHT CLOSE THE GATE
NINE, TEN DO IT AGAIN

b)
ALL OF OUR LIFE IS SPENT
DOING THINGS BY NUMBERS
DO THAT! DO THIS! NO, DON'T DO THAT
BUT DO EVERYTHING I SAY.
DO EVERYTHING I SAY

Verse 2:
SIT UP STRAIGHT
AND NEVER TALK WITH YOUR MOUTH FULL
WASH YOUR HANDS
AND LEAVE YOUR MUDDY SHOES OUTSIDE
THEY GO ON AND ONE AND TELL US WHAT WE
MUST DO.
IT'S ALWAYS THE SAME, WE'VE GOT TO DO WHAT
WE'RE TOLD.

Chorus: a)
ONE, TWO BUCKLE MY SHOE
THREE, FOUR SHUT THAT DOOR
FIVE, SIX, SEVEN, EIGHT CLOSE THE GATE
NINE, TEN DO IT AGAIN

b)
ALL OF OUR LIFE IS SPENT
DOING THINGS BY NUMBERS
DO THAT! DO THIS! NO, DON'T DO THAT!
DO EVERYTHING I SAY
DO EVERYTHING I SAY.

(Lights back on HEADMASTER and MISS GRANT who are busy examining the test papers).

ENTER NICHOLLS

HEADMASTER: Ah! there you are! Class, I want you to welcome Mr. Nicholls who is joining us this term and who will be teaching you English.

(MISS GRANT approaches HEADMASTER to hand him the rest of the test papers)

         And Mr. Nicholls, I'd like you to meet Miss Grant, our Drama mistress.

MISS GRANT: Pleased to meet you Mr. Nicholls.

NICHOLLS: My pleasure, Miss Grant.

HEADMASTER: *(distracted, flicking through test papers)* They're not a bad lot. Bit high-spirited, but they do their work. And I think you'll find that this school runs very smoothly. What! Here is a boy who has omitted to rule off at the end! *(Bears down on SMEETON)* Is this your paper, Smeeton?

SMEETON: Yes, Sir.

HEADMASTER: And what do we always say about ruling off, Smeeton?

SMEETON: Tidy work means a tidy mind, Sir.

HEADMASTER: That is correct. And to make sure you don't forget it I suggest you practise ruling off after school. You can rule me a line a mile long. I have previously calculated, purely from mild curiosity, that you will require one hundred and thirty-seven sheets of lined paper, which you will no doubt see fit to supply yourself. Mr. Nicholls, I believe we have already discussed the curriculum. Kindly continue with the lesson. Miss Grant will show you the book cupboard.

(HEADMASTER storms out)

MISS GRANT: Class, I don't want to hear another sound from you until Mr. Nicholls gets back.

(She beckons to NICHOLLS to follow her and they exit)

(The BOYS listen as they go. PLANK goes to the door, checks they really have gone, then signals the 'O.K.' to the others. He stands by the door, keeping 'cave'. The atmosphere relaxes. BROWN stands up, and mimics the HEADMASTER.

BROWN: I have previously calculated, purely from mild curiosity, that if you laid all Smeeton's relatives end to end, you could wrap them up in exactly one sheet of lined paper.

(General laughter)

(SMEETON has meanwhile begun his imposition. TUBBY, seated next to him, snatches the paper from his desk)

TUBBY: Got enough paper, Smeeton?

(SMEETON tries to hold on to the paper, and a fight ensues: SMEETON v. the rest)

(NICHOLLS enters, his arms full of books. He sees the fight, drops the books, and moves towards the BOYS to rescue SMEETON)

NICHOLLS: *(shouting)* Leave the boy alone, will you?

(Relative order is restored)

Are you alright?

SMEETON: Yes, Sir.

NICHOLLS: I may be a new teacher, but I don't like bullying, and I don't want any more of it. Now, *(To BROWN and COATES)* you two, come and help me with these books, will you?

(BROWN and COATES move to the spilt pile of books. COATES picks one up and looks at it)

COATES: Oh! No! not Dickens.

PLANK: We're always doing Dickens.

NICHOLLS: Just give the books out will you?

COATES: Can't we do something different, instead of reading books all the time?

BROWN: *(feigning stupidity)* Yeah, we could read comics for a change. Huh! Huh! Huh!

NICHOLLS: That's enough. What's your name?

BROWN: Brown, Sir.

NICHOLLS: Yes, well that's enough from you, Brown. Now, this book concerns the life of a young man called Nicholas Nickleby who loses his father . . .

BROWN: I wish my father would get lost.

(Sniggers)

NICHOLLS: *(pressing on)* . . . who loses his father and has to fend for himself.

TUBBY: Aaah! What a shame, eh, Smeeton? *(Flicks SMEETON on the ear)*

NICHOLLS: *(calmly furious, to TUBBY)* I'll see you afterwards. *(Continues)* In the first part of the story he is sent by his uncle to teach in a terrible school run by a mean grotesque old schoolmaster whose name is Squeers.

MARSH: Bit close to home, isn't it?

NICHOLLS: Compared to the pupils of that school you're well off — at least you've got enough to eat and you're not beaten every day. Can you picture having to live in that sort of school?

MARSH: Yeah, easily.

SMEETON: Imagine a school like that with our headmaster in it!

BOYS: Oh! Shut up! Smeeton.

NICHOLLS: Well, it might make everyone think a bit. So why don't we get on and read the book?

COATES: Who wants to read about another school? This one's bad enough.

BROWN: Why should we listen to you, anyway?

PLANK: No-one ever listens to us.

MARSH: Yeah, if you've got summink to say, you should be allowed to say it.

PLANK: Yeah, that's freedom of speech!

NICHOLLS: Then why don't you listen to me?

Song: "HERE I AM" (LOOKING FOR MY NAME)

NICHOLLS: YOU ASK ME WHAT EVERYTHING'S ABOUT
AND WHAT ON EARTH WE'RE DOING HERE.
I'VE NEWS FOR YOU, I'M LOOKING TOO
THE ANSWER ISN'T CLEAR.
BUT HERE I AM
LOOKING FOR MY NAME
DON'T UNDERSTAND.
SO HOW CAN I EXPLAIN.
STICK AROUND TILL WE HAVE FOUND
THE REASON WHY YOU AND I ARE HERE.

(As NICHOLLS sings, the BOYS' hostility changes to one of interest)

BOYS: HERE I AM
LOOKING FOR MY NAME
DON'T UNDERSTAND
SO HOW CAN I EXPLAIN
STICK AROUND TILL WE HAVE FOUND
THE REASON WHY YOU AND I ARE HERE.

NICHOLLS: IF YOU THINK YOU'VE GOT A BETTER SONG THAN
ME
THEN GO AHEAD AND SING.
AT LEAST THE TUNE I'M CALLING NOW
HAS GOT YOU FOLLOWING.

(By now the BOYS' resentment has vanished. As they sing they follow NICHOLLS' movements, and are now enjoying themselves)

BOYS: SO HERE I AM
LOOKING FOR MY NAME
DON'T UNDERSTAND.
SO HOW CAN I EXPLAIN.
STICK AROUND TILL WE HAVE FOUND
THE REASON WHY YOU AND I ARE HERE.
Da Da etc . . .

NICHOLLS: IF YOU THINK YOU'VE GOT A BETTER SONG THAN
ME
THEN GO AHEAD AND SING.
AT LEAST THE TUNE I'M CALLING NOW
HAS GOT YOU FOLLOWING.

BOYS: SO HERE I AM
LOOKING FOR MY NAME.
DON'T UNDERSTAND.
SO HOW CAN I EXPLAIN.
STICK AROUND TILL WE HAVE FOUND
THE REASON WHY YOU AND I ARE HERE.
Da Da etc . . .

(HEADMASTER and MISS GRANT enter)

HEADMASTER: What's all this noise going on? *(Looks around, pretends not to see NICHOLLS)* Who is in charge of this class? *(Feigns surprise)* Oh, there you are Nicholls. I will assume for the sake of your professional reputation that you were forced, momentarily, to leave the room, or that you were engaged on a dramatic reconstruction of the Battle of Waterloo.

MISS GRANT: As you can imagine, Headmaster, I find it impossible to conduct my class with this pandemonium going on next door.

HEADMASTER: You see Mr. Nicholls, you are making it very difficult for other members of the staff.

NICHOLLS: But it was only a bit of high spirits. We were just getting started.

HEADMASTER: In that case, it's just as well I interrupted before you finished.

(MISS GRANT twitters)

What possible justification can there be for this conduct, Mr. Nicholls.

NICHOLLS: Well actually Headmaster . . . we were . . . um . . . singing.

HEADMASTER: What?

NICHOLLS: Singing . . . making music.

HEADMASTER: What do you mean, making music? As far as I am aware this is an English lesson. You are supposed to be doing Nicholas Nickleby.

NICHOLLS: Exactly . . . we were doing Nicholas Nickleby . . . to music.

(CLASS looks incredulous)

HEADMASTER: I think you had better explain yourself, Nicholls.

NICHOLLS: We were . . . making Nicholas Nickleby into a musical. When you walked in, we were just about to give out the parts, weren't we?

(The CLASS are lost and shake their heads in bewilderment. NICHOLLS urges them to agree with him, so their head shaking turns to nods of agreement. The HEADMASTER looks at MISS GRANT with a puzzled expression)

MISS GRANT: Perhaps Headmaster, you haven't explained to Mr.

Nicholls, that I am the Drama Mistress at this school. Musical? I've never heard of such nonsense in all my life.

NICHOLLS: I'm merely trying to make English more interesting for them, by giving them a chance to express themselves.

HEADMASTER: Express themselves? Poppycock!

NICHOLLS: But shouldn't children enjoy learning?

(HEADMASTER calls NICHOLLS over to him. They and MISS GRANT move down stage leaving the children behind them in an excited cluster)

HEADMASTER: I don't think Mr. Nicholls, that having the children enjoy themselves is necessarily desirable. Getting them to sing with you is one thing. Earning their respect and obedience is another. Are you seriously suggesting that by singing your way through Nicholas Nickleby you are going to teach them anything?

MISS GRANT: I don't wish to seem patronising, Mr. Nicholls, but your approach to drama is somewhat naive.

NICHOLLS: And I don't wish to seem rude, Miss Grant, but do you have a better way?

MISS GRANT: I certainly do. And my way works!

NICHOLLS: Well, so will mine if you give me a chance.

MISS GRANT: Impossible!

HEADMASTER: *(breaking in)* No, Nicholls, I'm afraid it's quite out of the question.

NICHOLLS: *(sighs)* Oh well. It probably wouldn't have worked anyway. After all we would never have been able to find a dominant enough character for the leading role.

HEADMASTER: What's that?

NICHOLLS: Oh, the Headmaster of the school. A sensitively drawn character, crucial to the success of the musical. Of course one would need someone with quite remarkable talent to take the part. (He looks meaningfully at the HEADMASTER) Someone with a commanding presence, a certain air of authority, a man of decision, a man quite apart from the crowd. *(He turns and goes back to the children)*

HEADMASTER: *(moving towards the exit with MISS GRANT)* Miss Grant, I can see there would be certain advantages to Nicholls' idea . . .

(She looks at him amazed that he has been baited so easily)

    . . . educationally of course.

(She raises her eyebrows)

No, you're quite right. *(Turning to NICHOLLS)* I'm not entirely convinced, Mr. Nicholls, but your idea might just be feasible.

(CHILDREN cheer excitedly and gather in clusters)

Song: "STOP AND JUST THINK WHO YOU COULD BE"

BOYS:

GROUP 1:	STOP! AND JUST THINK WHO YOU COULD BE!
GROUP 2:	STOP! AND JUST THINK WHO YOU COULD BE!
GROUP 3:	STOP! AND JUST THINK WHO YOU COULD BE!
ALL:	STOP!

GROUP 1:	WHO'D PLAY THE PART OF SQUEERS THE HEAD-MASTER?
GROUP 2:	WHAT ABOUT YOU IN CHARGE OF US ALL SIR?
GROUP 1:	WHO'D PLAY THE PART OF FANNY HIS DAUGHTER?
GROUP 3:	SOMEBODY . . . MMM *(They point at MISS GRANT)* IT OUGHT TO BE HER.

GROUP 1:	STOP! AND JUST THINK WHO YOU COULD BE!
GROUP 2:	STOP! AND JUST THINK WHO YOU COULD BE!
GROUP 3:	STOP! AND JUST THINK WHO YOU COULD BE!
ALL:	STOP!

(The boys flick through their books to see what characters they can play)

COATES:	I WANNA BE COBBEY
MARSH:	I WANNA BE GRAYMARSH
BROWN:	I WANNA BE BOLDER
TUBBY:	I WANNA BE WACKFORD!

GROUP 1:	STOP! AND JUST THINK WHO YOU COULD BE!
GROUP 2:	STOP! AND JUST THINK WHO YOU COULD BE!
GROUP 3:	STOP! AND JUST THINK WHO YOU COULD BE!
ALL:	STOP!

EDITOR'S NOTE: n.b. alternative extra verse for production with mixed young people. See below:

GIRLS:	STOP! IT'S ALL ABOUT A BOYS' SCHOOL.
BOYS:	SO WHAT?
GIRLS:	SO WHAT ABOUT THE GIRLS THEN?
BOYS:	HOLD ON, WE'LL THINK OF SOMETHING FOR YOU.

(8 bar drum solo during which exciting dance routine could be presented)

Chorus	STOP! AND JUST THINK WHO YOU COULD BE! STOP!
ALL:	WHO'LL PLAY THE KID WHO'S LONELY AND OUTCAST?
SMEETON:	SMIKE?
ALL:	YOU!
SMEETON:	ME?
ALL:	YEA!
SMEETON:	NO!
ALL:	*(pointing at SMEETON)* SMIKE! SMIKE! SMIKE! SMIKE! SMIKE!
SMEETON:	*(speaking voice)* Alright! *(Turning to NICHOLLS)* But Sir, would you be Nickleby?

(During the number NICHOLLS and BOYS come down onto the apron)

(The stage area fades out ·for set change. Number ends with just NICHOLLS and SMEETON in two spots)

(Spot fades on NICHOLLS. SMEETON sings on his own: "STOP AND JUST THINK WHO YOU COULD BE." Spot gradually fades on him, as his voice fades into silence)

END OF SCENE

(Straight into transition music)

ACT ONE

TRANSITION

MUSICAL NUMBER

SCENE CHANGE

EDITOR'S NOTE: On the Programme Notes, it would be a good idea to explain that the Transition is from modern times to the 19th century, and that Squeers is in London recruiting pupils for Dotheboys Hall.

ACT ONE

Scene Two

THE SARACEN'S HEAD

Slide Screens could be used to establish scene and date.

SQUEERS is discovered. He is just over fifty, shortish and stout. He wears a patch over his left eye, an old black suit of the period, grubby linen. The jacket sleeves are too short. He is pacing up and down looking out of the window. The room is lit by two lamps either side of the fireplace, and a cheerful fire is in the grate. On the table are the remains of a meal, tankard etc. On the bench in the Left corner is a small trunk with a small BOY sitting on it. The child is obviously frightened. Two other small BOYS stand very dejected opposite the door.

SQUEERS: *(consulting his fob watch)* Half past three. There will be nobody here today. At midsummer I took down ten boys. Ten twenties is two hundred pounds. I go back at eight o'clock tomorrow morning and have only got three.

(He looks at the two BOYS by the fire, who have edged a little towards it, to warm themselves)

Cold are you?

1ST BOY: A little sir.

SQUEERS: Been living soft I'll be bound. No matter, we'll soon knock that out of you at Dotheboys. Now get back in the corner. Both of yer. Three boys. Three boys . . . three oughts is ought, three twos is six . . . sixty pounds. What's come of all the boys? What's parents got in their heads? What does it all mean?

(The BOY on the settle sneezes)

Hello sir, what's that, sir?

BOY: Nothing. Please sir.

SQUEERS: Nothing sir?

BOY: Please sir, I sneezed.

SQUEERS: Oh, sneezed did you? Then what did you say 'nothing' for, sir. *(Cuffs the BOY about the head)* Wait till I get you down into Yorkshire my Young Gentleman, and then I'll give you the rest. Will you hold your noise sir?

BOY: *(crying)* Y . . . yes.

SQUEERS: Then do so at once, sir. Do you hear?

(The BOY tries to stop crying and nods. RICHARD the waiter, enters through door UR)

RICHARD: *(coming down and clearing the meal things)* Mr. Squeers, there's a Gentleman asking for you at the bar.

SQUEERS: *(hastily sitting at the table and taking out a pen)* Show the Gentleman in, Richard.

(RICHARD takes the meal things and exits)

(to the BOY on the settle) Put your handkerchief in your pocket, you little scoundrel, or I'll murder you when the gentleman goes. *(Glances towards the door. With a changed manner)* My dear child, *(He pretends to write something)* all people have their trials. This early trial of yours, that is fit to make your little heart burst and your very eyes come out of your head with crying, what is it? Nothing, less than nothing.

(MR. SNAWLEY and his two SONS enter during this speech and stand watching SQUEERS from the doorway)

. . . You are leaving your friends, but you will have a father in me, and a mother in Mrs. Squeers. At the delightful little village of Dotheboys, near Greta Bridge, in Yorkshire, where youths are boarded, clothed, booked, washed, furnished with pocket money, provided with all necessaries . . .

SNAWLEY: It is the gentleman. Mr. Squeers I believe, sir?

SQUEERS: *(standing up and going to stand in front of the fire)* The same, sir.

SNAWLEY: The gentleman that advertised in the 'Times' newspaper?

SQUEERS: Morning Post, Chronicle, Herald and Advertiser, regarding the academy called Dotheboys Hall, at the delightful little village of Dotheboys, near Greta Bridge in Yorkshire. You come on business, I see sir, by my young friends. How do you do, my little gentlemen? And how do you do, sir?

(He pats the two BOYS on the head and holds his hand out to SNAWLEY who ignores it)

SNAWLEY: My name is Snawley, sir.

SQUEERS: *(dropping his hand)* And a very pretty name it is too.

SNAWLEY: I've been thinking, Mr. Squeers, of placing my two boys in your school.

SQUEERS: It is not for me to say sir, but I don't think you could possibly do better.

SNAWLEY: *(coughs)* Twenty pounds per annum, I believe, Mr. Squeers.

SQUEERS: Guineas.

SNAWLEY: Pounds for two, I think, Mr. Squeers.

SQUEERS: I don't think it could be done sir. Let me see. Four fives is twenty, double that and deduct the . . . well, a pound either way shall not stand betwixt us.

SNAWLEY: I thought that would be the case, Mr. Squeers. Seeing how we are both business men. Could I make as bold, Mr. Squeers, to ask for a few quiet words with you?

SQUEERS: By all means. *(To the BOYS)* My dears, will you speak with your new playfellows a moment or two. *(To SNAWLEY)* This is one of my boys, sir. *(He indicates the BOY on the settle)* Belling his name is, a Taunton boy that, sir.

SNAWLEY: Is he indeed.

SQUEERS: He goes along down with me tomorrow. That's his luggage that he's a-sittin' upon now. Not a very big parcel you may be thinking. But where's the sense in bringing lots of clothes when he's only going to grow out of 'em?

(They move below the fire. The BOYS have moved into a huddle around the BOY on the settle)

SNAWLEY:	The victuals at this Hall of yours, Mr. Squeers, must be very advantageous to a young boy's growth.
SQUEERS:	Oh indeed, they are. Indeed they are.

Song: "WE'VE GOT THE YOUNGSTERS' INTERESTS AT HEART"

SQUEERS:	WE'VE EVERY WHOLESOME LUXURY THAT YORK-SHIRE CAN AFFORD AND LOTS OF THINGS FOR THEM TO DO TO STOP THEM GETTING BORED.
SNAWLEY:	I STRONGLY WISH THEIR MORALS WILL BE ATTENDED TO
SQUEERS:	YOU KNOW I'VE GOT THEIR INTERESTS AT HEART EVERY COMFORT OF A HOME AWAITS THEM THERE THEY ALL RECEIVE THE SAME PARENTAL LOVE AND CARE AND THEN THERE'S MRS. SQUEERS, WHO'S MOTHER TO THEM ALL AND SHE WILL KNOW WHAT'S BEST FOR THEM AT DOTHEBOYS HALL.
Chorus 1:	WE'VE GOT THE YOUNGSTERS' INTERESTS AT HEART, YOU KNOW WE SEE TO IT THEY'RE TREATED AS THEY ARE AT HOME HOW COULD WE LIVE WITHOUT THEM OUR WORLD REVOLVES AROUND THEM WE'VE GOT THE YOUNGSTERS' INTERESTS AT HEART
SNAWLEY:	THAT'S SMART!
SQUEERS:	YES WE'VE GOT THE YOUNGSTERS' INTERESTS AT HEART.
SNAWLEY:	MAY I ASK AT WHAT AGE WILL THESE BOYS BE LEAVING SCHOOL?
SQUEERS:	UP TO ANY AGE YOU LIKE, THERE IS NO WRITTEN RULE. THE PROSPECTS OF THEM LEAVING US ARE VERY VERY LOW AND THAT'S OF COURSE A PLEASANT THING TO KNOW
SNAWLEY:	NO LETTERS SENT BACK HOME?

SQUEERS: EXCEPT AT CHRISTMAS TIME
AND THEN A CIRCULAR TO SAY THEY'RE FEELING
FINE
COS WE DO THINGS FOR THEM SIR, BELIEVE ME
THIS IS TRUE
THAT EVEN HALF THE MOTHERS GOING WOULD
NOT DO.

Chorus: WE'VE GOT THE YOUNGSTERS' INTERESTS AT
HEART YOU SEE
THIS HALL'S A HOME FROM HOME TO ALL WHO
COME TO ME
HOW COULD WE LIVE WITHOUT THEM
OUR WORLD REVOLVES AROUND 'EM
WE'VE GOT THE YOUNGSTERS' INTERESTS AT
HEART
YES WE'VE GOT THE YOUNGSTERS' INTERESTS AT
HEART.

SNAWLEY: I'M NOT THE BOYS' REAL FATHER, THEIR
MOTHER IS MY WIFE

SQUEERS: OUR SCHOOL WILL SOLVE YOUR PROBLEMS AND
WILL GIVE YOU PEACE FOR LIFE
NO EXTRAS, NO VACATIONS, THERE'S NOTHING
YOU NEED FEAR
FROM DOTHEBOYS HALL, NEAR GRETA BRIDGE
IN YORKSHIRE
BECAUSE WE'VE GOT THE YOUNGSTERS'
INTERESTS AT HEART YOU KNOW.

SQUEERS & SNAWLEY: Into repeat of Chorus 1

(At the end of the song SQUEERS and SNAWLEY both burst out laughing and slap each other on the back)

RICHARD enters UR.

RICHARD: Excuse me Gentlemen.

SQUEERS: Well?

RICHARD: There's another two gentlemen to see you, sir.

SQUEERS: *(pleased)* Well show them in. Show them in. No use keeping them waiting in the passage.

(RICHARD nods and exits)

SNAWLEY: *(taking a bag from his coat)* There remains, only Mr. Squeers, for me to give you this. *(He holds out the bag to SQUEERS)*

SQUEERS: *(with a small bow and a leer)* Mr. Snawley, you're a Gent.

(He takes the bag and they both laugh)

(RALPH NICKLEBY enters UR. He is a tall and stooped, elderly well dressed man. But we get the impression that he is not a nice man, for all his charm and good manners. He is followed by NICHOLAS NICKLEBY his nephew. A kind and generous young man in his early twenties)

(SQUEERS opens the bag and starts to count the coins)

RALPH: Mr. Squeers?

SQUEERS: *(hastily putting money in the bag and the bag in his pocket)* Here he is. *(He turns facing RALPH)* Oh, what is it I can do for you, sir?

RALPH: Only a matter of business, sir. There was an advertisement of yours in the morning paper.

SQUEERS: There was sir. This way if you please, sir.

(He shoos the BOYS into the corner and ushers RALPH and NICHOLAS on to the settle)

SQUEERS: Won't you be seated?

RALPH: Why, I think I will.

(He sits R end of the settle. He places his hat on the table. NICHOLAS stands above him)

This is my nephew, sir, Mr. Nicholas Nickleby.

SQUEERS: *(inclining his head)* How do you do, sir?

NICHOLAS: I'm ... I'm very well, thank you, sir.

RALPH: Perhaps you recollect me, sir.

SQUEERS: You paid me a small account at each of my half yearly visits to town, for some years, I think sir.

RALPH: I did.

SQUEERS: For the parents of a boy named Dorker, who unfortunately . . .

RALPH: Who unfortunately died at Dotheboys Hall.

SQUEERS: I remember very well sir. Ah, Mrs. Squeers, sir, was as partial to that boy as if he had been her own. The attention, sir, that was bestowed upon that boy in his illness! Dry toast and warm tea offered him every night and morning when he couldn't swallow anything, a candle in his room on the very night he died. The best dictionary sent up every night for him to lay his head on. I don't regret it though. It is a pleasant thing to reflect one did one's duty by him.

(RALPH smiles and nods)

(SNAWLEY who is nearly in tears also nods)

SQUEERS: *(indicating SNAWLEY who wipes his eye)* This gentleman, sir, is a parent who is kind enough to compliment me upon the course of education adopted at Dotheboys Hall, which is situated sir, at the delightful little village of Dotheboys near Greta Bridge in Yorkshire, where youths are boarded, booked, washed, furnished with pocket money . . .

RALPH: Yes, we know all that, sir. It's in the advertisement.

SQUEERS: You are very right, sir, it is in the advertisement.

SNAWLEY: And in the matter of fact besides, I feel bound to assure you, sir, and I am proud to have the opportunity of assuring you, that I consider Mr. Squeers a gentleman highly virtuous, exemplary, well educated, conducted and . . .

RALPH: *(cutting in)* I make no doubt of it, sir, no doubt of it at all. Suppose we come to business.

SQUEERS: With all my heart sir, never postpone business, is the very first lesson we teach our commercial pupils. Master Belling, my dear, always remember that, do you hear?

BELLING: *(stepping forward)* Yes sir.

RALPH: *(sarcastically)* He recollects what it is, does he?

SQUEERS: *(to prove his point)* Tell the gentleman.

BELLING: *(pause)* . . . Never . . .

SQUEERS: *(with a smile to RALPH)* Very good go on.

BELLING: *(pause)* . . . Never . . .

SQUEERS: Very good indeed, yes?

NICHOLAS: *(prompting)* Per . . .

BELLING:	P . . P . . . Perform . . . Business . . . Never-Perform-Business.
SQUEERS:	Very well sir. You and I will perform a little business on our own account, by and by.
RALPH:	And just now we had better transact our own business perhaps.
SQUEERS:	*(on his guard)* If you please.
RALPH:	Well it is brief enough, soon broached and I hope easily concluded. You advertised for an able assistant, sir.
SQUEERS:	*(relaxing)* Precisely so.
RALPH:	And you really want one.
SQUEERS:	Certainly.
RALPH:	Here he is. *(He indicates NICHOLAS)* My nephew Nicholas, hot from school with everything he learnt there fermenting in his head and nothing fermenting in his pockets, is just the man you want.
SQUEERS:	I'm afraid . . . I'm afraid your nephew won't suit me.
RALPH:	Yes he will. I know better. *(To NICHOLAS)* Don't be downcast, sir. You will be teaching all the young noblemen in Dotheboys Hall in less than a week's time, unless this gentleman is more obstinate than I take him to be.
NICHOLAS:	*(honestly)* I fear sir, that you object to my youth. And to my not being a master of arts.
SQUEERS:	The absence of a college degree is an objection.
RALPH:	Look here, sir. I'll put this matter in its true light, in a matter of two seconds.
SQUEERS:	If you'll have the goodness.
RALPH:	This is a boy or a youth or a lad or a young man or a hobbledehoy, or whatever you like to call him.
SQUEERS:	That I see.
SNAWLEY:	So do I.

(SQUEERS and RALPH glare at him)

RALPH: His father is dead, he is wholly ignorant of the world, has no resources whatever and wants something to do. I recommend him to this splendid establishment of yours as an opening which will lead him to fortune if he turns it to proper account. Do you see that?

NICHOLAS: I do, of course.

RALPH: *(rising and bringing SQUEERS down stage with him)* Let me have two words with you. The boy Dorker, died when?

SQUEERS: *(warily)* Just after Christmas.

RALPH: Exactly. And how many years was it before I was informed of his death?

SQUEERS: Years, Mr. Nickleby.

RALPH: Years, Mr. Squeers.

SQUEERS: *(making up his mind loudly)* Your uncle's recommendation has done it, Mr. Nickleby.

NICHOLAS: Then I am to be accepted?

RALPH: I think that can safely be assumed, don't you, Mr. Squeers.

SQUEERS: Your argument, sir, was very convincing. *(To NICHOLAS)* At eight o'clock tomorrow morning, Mr. Nickleby, the coach leaves. Be here a quarter before. Don't be late.

(Quick fade to Black)

END OF SCENE

Link Music.

Repeat trumpet section of
"WE'VE GOT THE YOUNGSTERS' INTERESTS AT HEART"

ACT ONE

Scene Three

OUTSIDE DOTHEBOYS HALL

Set: The railings from Scene 1. The nameboard has been changed to that of Dotheboys Hall. The stage is in darkness except for the railings, these are dimly lit. It is cold and a mist hangs in the air.

Link music continues from the last scene.

Into "SMIKE" Theme in minor key.

SQUEERS: *(Voice over)* Ah yes, Dotheboys Hall . . .

(Lights fade into scene as set. NICHOLAS is discovered stage right. He has a small travelling bag and is dressed in a heavy travelling coat)

      . . . situated in the delightful little village of Dotheboys, near Greta Bridge in Yorkshire, where youths are boarded, clothed, booked, washed, furnished with pocket money and provided with all necessaries.

RALPH: *(V.O.)* Perhaps you recollect me, sir?

SQUEERS: *(V.O.)* You paid me a small account at each of my half yearly visits to town, for some years, I think, sir.

RALPH: *(V.O.)* I did.

SQUEERS: *(V.O.)* For the parents of a boy named Dorker, who unfortunately . . .

RALPH: *(V.O.)* Who unfortunately died at Dotheboys Hall.

(A funeral bell slowly starts to toll)

(Lights come up on a small child's coffin. The coffin is carried shoulder high by BOYS who are on the stairs Left. We only see the coffin, no lights fall on the BOYS)

SQUEERS: *(V.O.)* I remember very well, sir . . .

(The school gates are opened by two URCHINS who stand with heads bowed. Lights fade up on MRS. SQUEERS, she is tall and gaunt with hands clasped in front of her. She appears grotesque in the light. Her face is hard and she has a very disagreeable expression)

      . . . Ah, Mrs. Squeers, sir . . .

(MRS. SQUEERS motions to the boys to hurry with the coffin as it is cold with the door open. The coffin moves slowly down the stairs)

SQUEERS: *(V.O.)* ... She was as partial to that boy, as if he had been her own ...

(The coffin has now reached MRS. SQUEERS. She snatches up a hat and scarf that are on top. MASTER SQUEERS appears from behind his mother's skirts. She wraps the scarf around his neck and puts the hat on his head)

... The attention that was bestowed upon that boy in his illness.

(Bell stops)

(MASTER SQUEERS snuggles into his scarf. MRS. SQUEERS looks smug)

... Dry toast and warm tea offered him every night and morning, when he couldn't swallow anything ...

(MRS. SQUEERS takes a bottle from her skirt and swigs from it)

(The BOYS move off with the coffin and slowly off Left)

... A candle in his bedroom on the very night he died ...

(Stair light snaps off)

(Two URCHINS close the gates and the stage lights fade, leaving us with only the railings visible)

... The best dictionary sent up for him to lay his head upon. I don't regret it though. It is a pleasant thing to reflect that one did one's duty by him ...

(End of music)

(Towards the end of the speech the voice fades)

(NICHOLAS takes a couple of steps towards the gates. He shudders and pulls his coat around him)

(SQUEERS enters Right)

SQUEERS: That's taken care of the new boys and the horses.

(NICHOLAS is hugging his coat tightly to him)

Are you cold, Nickleby?

NICHOLAS: *(starts)* Rather, sir, I must say.

SQUEERS: Well I don't find fault in that. It's been a long journey in this weather.

NICHOLAS: Indeed. So this is Dotheboys Hall, sir.

SQUEERS:	Hmm. *(He sucks at his teeth)* The fact is, it ain't a Hall.
NICHOLAS:	Oh, indeed.
SQUEERS:	No. We call it a Hall up in London because it sounds better, but they don't know it by that name in these parts. A man may call his house an island if he likes. There's no act of parliament against that I believe. *(Shouting towards the gates)* Hello there. Come and put this horse up. Be quick will yer, d'yer hear?
NICHOLAS:	I believe not sir.

(A candle appears at the top of the stairs L. It comes down towards the gates)

SQUEERS:	*(stamping his feet and muttering to himself)* Hmm, cold. Long way from London . . . Cold . . . Very long way . . . *(Suddenly yells)* Smike! Where the devil are yer?

(The gates are unlocked)

Is that you Smike?

(The gates are opened and we see SMIKE standing in the doorway. Dressed in rags he is a pathetic creature, small and thin and very lost)

SMIKE:	Yes sir.
SQUEERS:	Then why the devil didn't you come before?
SMIKE:	Please sir, I fell asleep over the fire.
SQUEERS:	*(grabbing hold of SMIKE by his shirt front)* Fire! What fire? Where's there a fire?
SMIKE:	Only in the kitchen, sir. Missis said as I was sittin' up I might as well go in there for a warm.
SQUEERS:	*(shaking SMIKE)* Your Missis is a fool, you'd have been a deuced deal more wakeful in the cold, I'll engage.
SMIKE:	Yes sir.
SQUEERS:	*(cuffing the boy's head and letting him go)* Now get out there and see to the luggage.

(SMIKE dashes off Right)

Come in Nickleby, come in. Welcome to Dotheboys Hall.

(Lights fade in on the SQUEERS' PARLOUR Right)

(Fly out railings)

END OF SCENE

ACT ONE

Scene Four

THE SQUEERS' PARLOUR.   DOTHEBOYS HALL

SQUEERS: Come on Nickleby, come in then, the wind blows in this door fit to knock a man off his legs.

(He leads the way over to the parlour. MRS. SQUEERS enters from the darkness Left. She has a steaming dish of food which hampers her embrace of SQUEERS. She is a tall and raw boned woman, full of energy and seems to bounce everywhere. She flings her arms round SQUEERS and plonks two kisses on each cheek. She is dressed in an old nightgown and has her hair in papers)

MRS. SQUEERS: Squeery! *(She embraces him)* And how is my Squeery? *(she goes to the dresser with the dish, not noticing NICHOLAS)*

SQUEERS: Quite well, my love. How are the cows?

MRS. SQUEERS: All right. Every one of them.

SQUEERS: And the pigs?

MRS. SQUEERS: As well as they were when you went.

SQUEERS: Come; that's a blessing. *(He takes off his coat)* The boys are all as they were I suppose?

MRS. SQUEERS: *(coming and taking the coat)*   Oh yes, they're well enough. That young Pitchers has a fever. *(She hangs the coat on the side of the dresser)*

SQUEERS: *(exploding)* No! Damn that boy, he's always at something of that sort.

MRS. SQUEERS: *(coming back to him)* Never was such a boy, I do believe. Whatever he has is always catching too. I say it's obstinacy, and nothing shall ever convince me that it isn't. I'd beat it out of him, and I told you that six months ago.

SQUEERS: *(touching her cheek)* So you did, my love, so you did. We'll try what can be done.

(She leers and nods)

This is the new young man, my dear.

MRS. SQUEERS: Oh. *(She turns and eyes NICHOLAS up and down and doesn't like what she sees)* Oh.

SQUEERS:	My dearest, this is Mr. Nickleby, who has come to be my assistant. Mr. Nickleby this is Mrs. Squeers, my very good wife.
NICHOLAS:	How do you do, Mrs. Squeers? I have heard many things of you from Mr. Squeers.
MRS. SQUEERS:	Has he eaten?
SQUEERS:	He'll take a meal with us tonight. You can give him a shakedown, in the corner, can't you?
MRS. SQUEERS:	We must arrange it somehow. You don't mind how you sleep, I suppose, sir?
NICHOLAS:	No, indeed, I'm not particular.
MRS. SQUEERS:	That's lucky.
SQUEERS:	*(yelling off Left)* Smike! . . . Smike bring those boxes from the trap and look sharp about it. *(To MRS. SQUEERS)* Before it slips my mind, my dear.
MRS. SQUEERS:	You think of everything. *(Kisses him)*
FANNY:	*(off Left)* Aoooow! You thieving brute, get in there.

(MASTER WACKFORD SQUEERS is flung into the room followed by FANNY)

	I'll bash yer head in. *(She grabs WACKFORD)*
MRS. SQUEERS:	Fanny!
FANNY:	I'll teach you to steal my pastry. *(Slaps him)*
SQUEERS:	Fanny!
FANNY:	You know I was doin' that special.

(He pushes her backwards and she stumbles into NICHOLAS)

NICHOLAS:	Miss Fanny?
FANNY:	Ooooo-er!
SQUEERS:	Our daughter Fanny, Mr. Nickleby.
NICHOLAS:	My pleasure, Miss Squeers.
FANNY:	Oh, hello.

(WACKFORD runs to MRS. SQUEERS)

MRS. SQUEERS:	And our son, Master Squeers.

NICHOLAS: Pleased to meet you sir.

(WACKFORD pulls a face)

MRS. SQUEERS: Fanny here, was so pleased to hear we was by way of having an assistant master, she did some baking for you.

NICHOLAS: That was very kind. I do hope you have not inconvenienced yourself, Miss Squeers.

FANNY: Course not.

SQUEERS: *(fondly indicating MRS. SQUEERS, FANNY and WACKFORD)* Well, Nickleby, there's a picture for you. What d'you think of them?

NICHOLAS: *(at a loss for words)* Very fine sir.

SQUEERS: You won't see such a family as this very often I think. I should like to know how I should ever get on without them.

Song: "WACKFORD, FANNY, SQUEERSY
AND ME" (Quartet)

SQUEERS: *(indicating MRS. SQUEERS)*
A MOST INVALUABLE WOMAN
A MOTHER TO 'EM ALL.
A COMFORT AND A JOY TO ALL THE BOYS SIR,
THE PRIDE OF DOTHEBOYS HALL.
THAT WOMAN NEVER CHANGES,
SHE MEANS SO MUCH TO ME.
THE VERY FIRST TIME WE MET, I LOVED
THAT BUSTLING, LIVELY CREATURE YOU SEE.

Chorus: WE'RE ONE LITTLE FAMILY
PARTNERS IN CHARITY
AND WE'LL GO FAR
WE ALL LIVE HAPPILY
WACKFORD, FANNY

MRS. SQUEERS: *(as she puts her arm round MR. SQUEERS)*
SQUEERSY AND ME.

MRS. SQUEERS: *(indicating WACKFORD)*
THIS IS OUR INFANT PHENOMENON,
YORKSHIRE BORN AND BRED,
A SPECIMEN OF PERFECT GASTRONOMY
WITH ALL THE THINGS HE'S FED.
THE IDOL OF HIS MUM AND PAPA
A BLESSING TO US ALL.
THERE'S FLESH ON HIM FOR TWENTY BOYS, SIR.
YOU COULDN'T FIND BETTER AT DOTHEBOYS
HALL.

Chorus:	WE'RE ONE LITTLE FAMILY PARTNERS IN CHARITY AND WE'LL GO FAR WE ALL LIVE HAPPILY WACKFORD, FANNY,
MRS. SQUEERS:	SQUEERSY AND ME

(SQUEERS looks on dotingly)

WACKFORD:	ONE DAY WHEN I GROW UP TO BE A BIGGER BOY I WILL RUN THIS SCHOOL, OH MY EYE WON'T I GIVE IT TO ALL THE BOYS. I'LL LAY DOWN THE RULES. THEY'LL WISH THAT THEY COULD TURN THE CLOCKS BACK WHEN PAPA'S RETIRED. I'LL KEEP THE FAMILY TRADITION AND LIVE OFF THE FAT OF THE BOYS IN THE HALL.
Chorus:	WE'RE ONE LITTLE FAMILY PARTNERS IN CHARITY AND WE'LL GO FAR WE ALL LIVE HAPPILY WACKFORD, FANNY,
MRS. SQUEERS:	SQUEERSY AND ME.
Chorus:	Pa Pa etc De Da etc
FANNY:	ONE DAY I'D LIKE TO BE A LADY THE BELLE OF DOTHEBOYS HALL. A CHARMING PRINCE WOULD COME AND FALL IN LOVE WITH ME AND TAKE ME TO THE BALL. WE'D SETTLE DOWN AND RAISE OUR CHILDREN THE WAY THEY OUGHT TO BE. MA AND PA WOULD FEEL SO PROUD WHEN WE CAME OVER TO SEE THEM AT DOTHEBOYS HALL
Chorus:	WE'D BE ONE LITTLE FAMILY PARTNERS IN CHARITY AND WE'D GO FAR WE'D ALL LIVE HAPPILY WACKFORD, FANNY, SQUEERSY AND ME La La etc YES WE ALL LIVE HAPPILY WACKFORD, FANNY SQUEERSY AND ME.
SQUEERS:	Well, now you have met my happy family, Mr. Nickleby, perhaps we can get down to the business which brought you to this part of the world.

NICHOLAS: I'm very much looking forward to meeting the boys, sir.

SQUEERS: *(sucks his teeth)* Hmmmmm.

(SMIKE enters left)

SMIKE: Sir.

SQUEERS: What, boy? What brings you here?

SMIKE: I've brought the trunks, if you please sir.

SQUEERS: And not before time. Well, don't stand there like a fool,
                 bring 'em in.

SMIKE: Yes, sir.

NICHOLAS: I'll give you a hand.

SQUEERS: Mr. Nickleby . . . He don't need no help . . .

(SMIKE exits Left)

                 He's pleased to do it. It warms his little heart to think
                 he's helping.

NICHOLAS: They did look rather heavy.

SQUEERS: All the better, uses up his energy, stops him gettin' up to
                 mischief.

(SMIKE enters with a trunk)

MRS. SQUEERS: *(indicating the table)* Put it here.

(SMIKE crosses to the table, puts down the trunk and exits. MRS. SQUEERS holds out her hand and SQUEERS tosses her the trunk keys. She opens the trunk and starts taking out clothing and holds it up to MASTER SQUEERS)

SQUEERS: Come, Nickleby.

(Lights come up on the stairs left. SQUEERS crosses with NICHOLAS following and they mount the stairs and exit)

(MRS. SQUEERS continues to sort through the trunk)

(FANNY stands and stares at NICHOLAS)

(All lights fade to BLACK)

ACT ONE

Scene Five

SCHOOLROOM. DOTHEBOYS HALL

Lights fade into Schoolroom. The BOYS are discovered, they look more like sewer rats than human beings. SQUEERS' voice can be heard talking to NICHOLAS. The BOYS freeze and look up at the door, they are afraid to move. The door opens and SQUEERS and NICHOLAS enter. The BOYS rush to their places. SQUEERS bangs on the balustrade with a cane.

SQUEERS: Go on, get to your desks.

(The BOYS finish getting to their places and watch SQUEERS descend to the platform)

Boys, I want you to welcome Mr. Nickleby, the son of a gentleman, newly come from London with me to help with your upbringing and moral education. Say hello nicely boys.

BOYS: *(in spiritless monotone)* Good evening, Mr. Nickleby.

(NICHOLAS nervously nods his head)

SQUEERS: You also have five new playfellows, show them where everything is boys . . .

(The five NEW BOYS now dressed in rags are clustered together frightened out of their lives. The BOYS (class) start to move to show the NEW BOYS where to go).

Not now, later.

(The BOYS stop in their tracks. MRS. SQUEERS and FANNY enter at the top of the steps. MRS. SQUEERS has a huge jug, FANNY a tray with a jug of beer)

SQUEERS: *(seeing MRS. SQUEERS)* Ah, my own dear wife and her little help-mate. She's a great comfort to me and a mother to the boys. She's more than a mother to them, ten times more. She does things for them, Nickleby, that I don't believe half the mothers going would do for their own sons.

(BOYS nod in sarcastic agreement)

(MRS. SQUEERS has come down into the room with FANNY. They place their jugs on the top desk)

(*picking up his jug of beer*) A most invaluable woman that, Nickleby. (*He takes a swig of beer*)

NICHOLAS: Indeed, sir.

SQUEERS: I do not know her equal, I just do not know her equal. That woman, Nickleby, is always the same - same bustling, lively, active, saving creature that you see her. A real mother to the boys, and what they lack in material comforts we make up for in love and charity.

(CUE INTRO for song: "DOTHEBOYS HALL")

Love and charity, Mr. Nickleby, love and charity.

(He has come down the steps to join MRS. SQUEERS)

Song: "DOTHEBOYS HALL"

SQUEERS: DOTHEBOYS HALL IS A VERY NICE HALL
AND A VERY NICE PLACE TO BE.

(BOYS shake their heads in vigorous disagreement)

THEY'VE GOT A MOTHER FIGURE IN MRS.
                    SQUEERS
AND A FATHER FIGURE IN ME.
WE CLOTHE, BOARD, BOOK, WASH
LIKE SONS OF NOBILITY
AT DOTHEBOYS HALL NEAR GRETA BRIDGE IN
                    YORKSHIRE.

BOYS: *(sung ironically)*
THEY CLOTHE, BOARD, BOOK, WASH
THE SONS OF NOBILITY.
AT DOTHEBOYS HALL NEAR GRETA BRIDGE
WE LIVE IN HARMONY.

MRS. SQUEERS: ROAST TURKEY, BEEF, COLD HAM AND TONGUE

(BOYS lean forward hungrily)

MAKE UP OUR DAY'S SUBSISTENCE
THE BOYS DON'T NEED TO TASTE IT,

(Then slump back disappointedly)

THEY JUST SMELL IT FROM A DISTANCE.

SQUEERS: WE GUIDE 'EM, MIND 'EM, LEARN 'EM, LOVE 'EM,
LIKE OUR VERY OWN FAMILY.
AT DOTHEBOYS HALL NEAR GRETA BRIDGE IN
                    YORKSHIRE.

BOYS: THEY GUIDE, MIND, LEARN, LOVE
THEIR VERY OWN FAMILY.
AT DOTHEBOYS HALL NEAR GRETA BRIDGE
WE LIVE IN HARMONY.

BOYS: DOTHEBOYS HALL IS A VERY NICE HALL
AND A VERY NICE PLACE TO BE.
'COS TATTERED RAGS AND HUNGER MAKE
FOR MORAL PURITY.

(They shake their fists to demonstrate the double entendre of the next line)

BOYS: WE WON'T FORGET THE THINGS THEY DONE
IN CHRISTIAN CHARITY.
AT DOTHEBOYS HALL NEAR GRETA BRIDGE IN
                    YORKSHIRE.

SQUEERS &   THEY WON'T FORGET THE THINGS WE DONE
MRS. SQUEERS: IN CHRISTIAN CHARITY.
AT DOTHEBOYS HALL NEAR GRETA BRIDGE
WE LIVE IN HARMONY.

(The last word, 'harmony' is sung out of tune. The BOYS boo)

SQUEERS: IF ANYBODY RUNS AWAY
WE VERY QUICKLY SPOT 'EM.

MRS. SQUEERS: WE ASK 'EM WHAT THE PROBLEM IS
BECAUSE WE'VE NOT FORGOTTEN.

BOTH: THAT THE WAY TO SOLVE ALL PROBLEMS IS
TO START RIGHT AT THE BOTTOM.

(SQUEERS swishes one of the BOYS on the backside)

                AT DOTHEBOYS HALL NEAR GRETA BRIDGE
IN YORKSHIRE.

BOYS: THE WAY TO SOLVE ALL PROBLEMS IS
TO START RIGHT AT THE BOTTOM.
AT DOTHEBOYS HALL NEAR GRETA BRIDGE
WE LIVE IN HARMONY.

SQUEERS: Christian Charity and good wholesome diet, that's what the boys enjoy at Dotheboys Hall. There's many that would be thankful for a good wholesome diet. You appreciate, Mr. Nickleby, that the boys love their food — don't you boys?

(BOYS nod vigorously)

NICHOLAS: Indeed sir. It would seem they cannot get enough of it.

SQUEERS: You are right, Mr. Nickleby, and very greedy little tykes some of them are too. You will observe, my dear sir, the looks of anticipation among their little faces, as my dear little help-mate lays the evening meal.

(FANNY is putting a jug on each desk)

NICHOLAS: And what are they to eat, sir?

SQUEERS: Milk, Mr. Nickleby.

NICHOLAS: Milk and what, sir?

SQUEERS: Milk and water, sir. At two penn'orth a quart would you beggar me sir?

NICHOLAS: But I only enquire as to . . .

SQUEERS: Ah! *(Cutting in)* Here's richness. *(Looks into the milk jug given to him by MRS. SQUEERS)* Think of the many beggars and orphans in the streets that would be glad of this, little boys. A shocking thing hunger is, Mr. Nickleby.

NICHOLAS: Very shocking, sir.

SQUEERS: When I say number one, the first boy in each line may take a drink; and when I say number two, the next boy may, and so on until the last boy, are you ready?

(Instrumental verse as milk is passed round. SQUEERS sings "One, two, three, four, five" as each BOY comes to his turn. BOYS move away from MR. AND MRS. SQUEERS after receiving their milk)

Song: "DOING THINGS BY NUMBERS"
(REPRISE)

Chorus:
ALL OF OUR LIFE IS SPENT
DOING THINGS BY NUMBERS
DO THAT! DO THIS! NO, DON'T DO THAT!
BUT DO EVERYTHING I SAY,
DO EVERYTHING I SAY.

JOIN THE QUEUE
AND WAIT TILL THEY CALL YOUR NUMBER
HOW D'YOU DO?
TELL ME YOUR NUMBER AND NAME.
WE'RE LIVING IN THE KIND OF WORLD WHERE IT
PAYS TO BE OLD.
WE'RE PUSHED AROUND, AND JUST LIKE CLOWNS
WE DO WHAT WE'RE TOLD

Chorus: a)   ONE, TWO BUCKLE MY SHOE
                      THREE, FOUR SHUT THAT DOOR
                      FIVE, SIX, SEVEN, EIGHT CLOSE THE GATE
                      NINE, TEN DO IT AGAIN

           b)   ALL OF OUR LIFE IS SPENT
                      DOING THINGS BY NUMBERS
                      DO THAT! DO THIS! NO, DON'T DO THAT
                      BUT DO EVERYTHING I SAY
                      DO EVERYTHING I SAY.

MRS. SQUEERS: Right boys, time for bed, and if I hear so much as a sound, Mr. Squeers will give you so much of a beating you won't wake up in the morning. *(She turns to SQUEERS)* Come on dearie, we must eat. *(To NICHOLAS)* You'd better come with us, Mr. Knuckle-boy.

(Lights fade to BLACK)

ACT ONE

Scene Six

THE SQUEERS' PARLOUR. DOTHEBOYS HALL

*Discovered: FANNY making eyes at NICHOLAS throughout. SQUEERS.
MRS. SQUEERS, MASTER SQUEERS, NICHOLAS, FANNY, seated round
a table, eating.*

MRS. SQUEERS: Smike! Smike! Where the devil is that boy? Smike!
Bah! Can't you hurry, I want you.

SQUEERS: Where is the wretched boy? *(He stands)* Smike!

(SMIKE enters Left)

MRS. SQUEERS: And where do you think you've been, my fine feathered
friend?

SMIKE: I was at the pump, please Missis.

SQUEERS: You took your time, get me some ale and be quick about
it.

SMIKE: Yes, sir.

*(SQUEERS has a bundle of letters. SMIKE moves up to him and stands
looking at them)*

MRS. SQUEERS: What are you standing there bothering for?

SMIKE: *(to SQUEERS)* Please sir . . .

SQUEERS: Well?

SMIKE: Have you . . . Did anybody . . . Has nothing been heard
about me?

SQUEERS: The devil take you. Not a word and never will be. Now
be off with you and bring me that ale, be sharpish about
it.

(SMIKE sadly exits)

    . . . Now there's a pretty sort of thing, ay, Nickleby.

NICHOLAS: Why does he ask, 'has nothing been heard about me?"

SQUEERS:	Why, 'cause he's been here all these years and no money paid after the first six months, nor no notice taken, nor no clue to be got as to who he belongs. It's a pretty sort of thing that I should have to clothe and feed a fellow like him, and never hope to get a penny for it. *(He tucks into his meal)*
MRS. SQUEERS:	How's the beefsteak, Squeersy?
SQUEERS:	Tender as a lamb, my love, an uncommon juicy meal. Will you not join me?
MRS. SQUEERS:	I couldn't eat a morsel. What'll the young man take, my dear?
SQUEERS:	Whatever he likes that's present. Smike! Smike! Where is the boy? Smike! Bring the ale.
MRS. SQUEERS:	What do you say, Mr. Knuckleboy? A little of our Fanny's pie.

(FANNY leers)

NICHOLAS:	*(with a smile at FANNY)* I'll take a little of the pie, if you please. A very little, for I am not hungry.
MRS. SQUEERS:	Well 'tis a pity to cut the pie, if you're not hungry, isn't it?

(FANNY glares at her mother)

Will you try a bit of the beef?

NICHOLAS:	Whatever you please, it's all the same to me.
SQUEERS:	Uncommon juicy steak that. *(He wipes the back of his sleeve across his mouth, sniffs, pats his stomach and belches)*
MRS. SQUEERS:	Well it were prime meat that. I bought extra large piece on purpose for . . .
SQUEERS:	For what? Not for the boys?
MRS. SQUEERS:	No! On purpose for you, against you should come home. You don't think I'd ever make a mistake as that.
SQUEERS:	Upon my word, my dear. I didn't know what you were going to say.
MRS. SQUEERS:	You needn't make yourself uncomfortable, to think that I should be such a noddy.

SQUEERS: *(to NICHOLAS who is staring at his food)* Let that be a lesson to you, Mr. Nickleby. You seem somewhat disturbed sir. Out with it, there are no secrets here at Dotheboys Hall.

NICHOLAS: I was merely reflecting that whilst we eat, there are so many who go without.

MRS. SQUEERS: *(viciously)* Meaning by that, I suppose . . .

SQUEERS: *(cutting in)* Now let's not be hasty, my dear. *(He rounds on NICHOLAS)* Sir, this is the essence of our discipline at Dotheboys. Our society is a privileged one, our young charges will one day hold privileged positions themselves, but before they can hold it wisely they must learn to see it in action. That *(He leans back)* is good domestic economy.

(SMIKE enters)

Well what do you want?

SMIKE: Please sir, I've brought the ale.

SQUEERS: Oh, so you've brought the ale have you? You've been a long time. You're a lazy boy.

(SMIKE advances with the ale)

(SQUEERS advances on SMIKE who cowers away)

SMIKE: Please sir, I had to open a new cask.

SQUEERS: *(hits SMIKE with a cane that he has just picked up)* You're a lazy boy . . . I'll learn you to know your place. You're lazy . . . lazy . . . lazy . . . lazy . . . lazy.

(He hits SMIKE each time he says it, until SMIKE is left in a heap on the floor)

Now get to your bed.

(He delivers a kick to SMIKE as he crawls out sobbing)

SQUEERS: Some more meat, Nickleby?

NICHOLAS: Er, no, I don't think I feel like any more.

MRS. SQUEERS: Gone off his food has he?

SQUEERS: Well suit yourself.

MRS. SQUEERS: Come on dearie, I'm tired.

SQUEERS: We'll put you in your regular bedroom tomorrow, Nickleby. Now let me see, who sleeps in Brooks' bed, my dear?

MRS. SQUEERS: *(yawning)* In Brooks'? Well there's Jennings, little Bolder, Graymarsh and little what's 'is name.

SQUEERS: So there is, then Brooks's full.

NICHOLAS: Full!! I should think it was.

SQUEERS: There's a place somewhere, I know, but I can't at this moment call to mind where it is. However we'll have that settled tomorrow.

MRS. SQUEERS: You'll find a little bit of soap in the kitchen window. That belongs to you. I don't know whose towel to put you on but if you'll makeshift with something tomorrow morning I'll arrange something in the course of the day.

SQUEERS: Don't forget, my dear.

MRS. SQUEERS: I'll take care. *(To NICHOLAS)* And mind you take care young man and get first wash. The teacher should always have it, but they'll try and get the better of you if they can.

SQUEERS: *(walking Left with MRS. SQUEERS)* You can bed yourself down in here for the night, Nickleby. We'll make more permanent arrangements for you in the morning . . .

(MRS. SQUEERS walks back to the table, picks up the jug of ale and carries it off with her)

SQUEERS: . . . Good night then Nickleby, six o'clock in the morning mind, and I'll show you myself where the pump is for you to wash.

(He exits Left with MRS. SQUEERS on his arm)

(NICHOLAS looks around him and goes to the carver chair and pulls it forward a little. He stops and listens)

(Lights dim on NICHOLAS and go up on SMIKE who is huddled at the bottom of the stairs L)

(SMIKE, unaware of NICHOLAS, sings)

Song: "BETTER OFF THE WAY I AM"

SMIKE:
NEVER HAD A MUM OR DAD TO CALL MY OWN
BUT IT'S FUNNY HOW YOU NEVER MISS THE
    THINGS YOU'VE NEVER KNOWN
'THOUGH SOMETHING IN MY LIFE HAS GONE
    THAT NEVER CAME
EVERYTHING THAT I'VE LOST HAS GOT TO BE MY
    GAIN.

Chorus:
PARENTS, WHAT KIND OF PEOPLE DO THEY
    THINK THEY ARE
THAT I SHOULD HAVE TO OWE THEM MY LIFE
    AND NOTHING MORE
I'M REALLY GLAD THEY DIDN'T CARE
'COS WHO NEEDS PEOPLE TELLING YOU
TO GO TO BED AND SAY YOUR PRAYERS
CLEAN YOUR TEETH AND GET UPSTAIRS
OOH BY GOLLY I'M BETTER OFF THE WAY I AM

SMIKE:
WHO CAN SAY I'M RIGHT OR WRONG TO FEEL
    THIS WAY
I WOULDN'T GIVE THE TIME OF DAY TO PARENTS
    ANYWAY
NOTHING YOU CAN DO OR SAY WILL CHANGE MY
    MIND
EVERYTHING I'VE SEEN OF LIFE IS KILLING ME
    INSIDE

Chorus:
PARENTS, WHAT KIND OF PEOPLE DO THEY
    THINK THEY ARE
IT'S JUST A WORD FOR LOVERS WHO BRING YOU
    IN THE WORLD
AND THEN THE LOVING STARTS TO FADE
WHO NEEDS PEOPLE MAKING YOU
DRESS UP IN YOUR SUNDAY CLOTHES
COMB YOUR HAIR AND BLOW YOUR NOSE
OOH BY GOLLY I'M BETTER OFF THE WAY I AM

Repeat First Chorus

(Song ends. Lights go up on NICHOLAS. He approaches SMIKE)

NICHOLAS: Smike!

(SMIKE cowers away)

You need not fear me. I won't hurt you. Are you cold?

SMIKE: N . . . N . . No.

NICHOLAS: *(taking off his jacket)* You're shivering.

SMIKE: I'm not cold. I'm used to it.

NICHOLAS: Here, put this round you.

(SMIKE comes to him and NICHOLAS puts his jacket round the boy)

SMIKE: Do you remember the boy that died here?

NICHOLAS: I was not here, you know. But what of him?

SMIKE: Why, I was with him at night and when it was all silent he cried no more for friends he wished to come and sit with him, but began to see faces round his bed that had come from home; he said they smiled and talked to him; and he died at last lifting his head to kiss them. Do you hear?

NICHOLAS: Yes . . . Yes, I hear.

SMIKE: Who will talk to me in those long nights? What faces will smile on me when I die? You think you can help me, but you can't, no one can, no one can find my father and mother. No hope . . .

(CUE INTRO for song: "DON'T LET LIFE GET YOU DOWN")

. . . There's no hope.

NICHOLAS: Ssssssssh, when I look at this wretched school I feel as un-happy as you, but we must both say, there's always hope.

Song: "DON'T LET LIFE GET YOU DOWN"

NICHOLAS:
PEOPLE THINK THEY SEE A MOUNTAIN
BUT IT'S JUST A LITTLE HILL.
AND THE PROBLEMS THAT SURROUND THEM
ARE JUST THE MOOD THEY FEEL.
BUT DANGERS IN THE DARKNESS
ARE ONLY IN YOUR MIND
BETTER KEEP YOUR EYES WIDE OPEN
LOOK AROUND.

BOYS
& NICHOLAS: *(offstage)*
DON'T LET LIFE GET YOU DOWN
EVEN THOUGH THE WORLD MIGHT LET YOU
                                    DOWN.
DON'T LET LIFE
DON'T LET LIFE
DON'T LET LIFE GET YOU DOWN.

(BOYS enter upstage in formation, each holding a candle)

NICHOLAS: IF YOU THINK THAT YOU'RE A LOSER
YOU'RE NEVER GOING TO WIN.
YOU'LL NEVER CHANGE YOUR SITUATION
UNLESS YOU THINK AND THEN BEGIN.
SO GET UP, GO ON, GO EVERYWHERE
AND CLOUDS WILL LEAVE YOUR MIND.
COS THE ONLY ONE TO MAKE IT WILL BE YOU.

BOYS: DON'T LET LIFE GET YOU DOWN
EVEN THOUGH THE WORLD MIGHT LET YOU
DOWN
COS DANGERS IN THE DARKNESS
ARE ONLY IN YOUR MIND
BETTER KEEP YOUR EYES WIDE OPEN
LOOK AROUND.
DON'T LET LIFE GET YOU DOWN
EVEN THOUGH THE WORLD MIGHT LET YOU
DOWN.
DON'T LET LIFE
DON'T LET LIFE
DON'T LET LIFE GET YOU DOWN.

IF YOU THINK YOU'RE A LOSER
YOU'RE NEVER GOING TO WIN.
YOU'LL NEVER CHANGE YOUR SITUATION
UNLESS YOU THINK AND THEN BEGIN.
SO GET UP, GO ON, GO EVERYWHERE
AND CLOUDS WILL LEAVE YOUR MIND
COS THE ONLY ONE TO MAKE IT WILL BE YOU.

BOYS
& NICHOLAS: DON'T LET LIFE GET YOU DOWN.
EVEN THOUGH THE WORLD MIGHT LET YOU
DOWN.
COS DANGERS IN THE DARKNESS
ARE ONLY IN YOUR MIND
BETT ER KEEP YOUR EYES WIDE OPEN
LOOK AROUND.
DON'T LET LIFE GET YOU DOWN
EVEN THOUGH THE WORLD MIGHT LET YOU
DOWN.
DON'T LET LIFE
DON'T LET LIFE
DON'T LET LIFE GET YOU DOWN.

(SMIKE and NICHOLAS move downstage)

(Tabs close slowly as SMIKE Theme plays)

END OF ACT ONE

Interval

MUSIC

ACT TWO

1. DAWN MUSIC

   into

   IN THE WARM LIGHT OF A BRAND NEW DAY

2. DOTHEBOYS ROCK

3. BRIMSTONE AND TREACLE

4. YOUR KIND OF WOMAN

5. WE'LL FIND OUR DAY

6. HERE I AM

7. DON'T LET LIFE GET YOU DOWN / IN THE WARM LIGHT

8. BELIEVE

9. Reprise   DOTHEBOYS ROCK

ACT TWO

Scene One

DOTHEBOYS HALL

Classroom

The music starts while the houselights are up. The houselights dim slowly to BLACK.

Stage is set in darkness. The classroom is now being used as a dorm. BOYS are sleeping everywhere, SMIKE is asleep Right. The tabs open and a choir (BOYS) begins to hum.

On music cue a light breaks through a window set high up in the wall Left. A small shaft of light falls on to SMIKE who wakes.

Song: "IN THE WARM LIGHT OF A BRAND NEW DAY"

SMIKE'S isolation from the other BOYS is now over and later they join in the song. Towards the end of the song NICHOLAS enters down the stairs and watches the BOYS.

Song: "IN THE WARM LIGHT OF A BRAND NEW DAY"

SMIKE:
        TODAY HAS COME
        I SEE THE SUN
        IT'S SHINING EVERYWHERE.
        A CHANGE OF HEART
        HAS JUST BEGUN
        THE SILVER LINING'S THERE.
        AND WHEN I'M FEELING LOST
        I'LL KEEP MY FINGERS CROSSED
        AND TRY TO SHOW THAT I DON'T CARE.
        IN THE WARM LIGHT OF A BRAND NEW DAY . . .

        I FOUND A LONG LOST HAPPINESS
        WHEN I WOKE UP TODAY.
        THE COLD I FELT INSIDE OF ME
        CAN NOW BE PUSHED AWAY.
        COS WHEN I'M FEELING LOST
        I'LL KEEP MY FINGERS CROSSED
        AND TRY TO SHOW THAT I DON'T CARE
        IN THE WARM LIGHT OF A BRAND NEW DAY . . .
        La La etc . . .

FOR JUST ONE MOMENT IN MY LIFE
I NEEDN'T RUN AWAY.
THIS PASSING MOOD OF HAPPINESS
WILL HELP ME FACE THE DAY.
AND WHEN I'M FEELING LOST
I'LL KEEP MY FINGERS CROSSED
AND TRY TO SHOW THAT I DON'T CARE.
IN THE WARM LIGHT OF A BRAND NEW DAY . . .

The song ends.

VOICE OFF: What's all this noise going on in 'ere?

(The BOYS scatter, terrified that it is Squeers. A huge shadow of a person with a stick, appears on the facing wall Left. Below the stairs the BOYS cower in silence. BOLDER enters at the top of the stairs, mimicking SQUEERS. He comes down amid general laughter)

Song: "DOTHEBOYS ROCK"

INTRO: I'M MR. SQUEERS AND I RUN THIS SCHOOL
  BOLDER:–   YOU'VE GOT NOTHING TO FEAR FROM ME AS
                     LONG AS YOU KEEP MY RULES.

(changes his voice and now pretends to sing TO Mr. Squeers)

           HEY THERE MISTER, YOU'RE GETTING REAL
                 SORT OF KINDA OLD
           AND ONE OF THESE DAYS WE'RE GONNA RUN
                 AMOK AND GO FOR GOOD OLD ROCK & ROLL

Verse 1:   I WAS DANCING WITH MATILDA AT THE BREAK
                 OF DAWN
           WE WERE HAVING PLENTY FUN TILL OLD
                 SQUEERSY CAME ALONG WO YEH,
           SEE THE BOYS ROCKIN'
           DO THE BOYS ROCK, DO THE BOYS ROCK AND
                 ROLL?

Verse 2:   GONNA TELL PAPA BOLDER 'BOUT DOTHEBOYS
                 HALL
           THE MONEY SENT TO FEED US DON'T GET TO US
                 AT ALL WO YEH,
           REELIN' AND A ROCKIN'
           DO THE BOYS ROCK, DO THE BOYS ROCK AND
                 ROLL?

Chorus:
DO THE BOYS ROCK YEH YEH
DO THE BOYS ROLL YEH YEH
DO THE BOYS ROCK YEH YEH
DO THE BOYS ROLL YEH YEH
DO THE BOYS ROCK, DO THE BOYS ROCK AND
    ROLL

Verse 3:
SQUEERSY'S GOT A DAUGHTER ONLY FOUR FOOT
    FIVE
BUT MAN YOU OUGHTA SEE HER WHEN SHE HITS
    THAT JIVE OH YEH
REELIN' AND A ROCKIN'
DO THE BOYS ROCK, DO THE BOYS ROCK AND
    ROLL?

Verse 4:
WHEN I'M SITTING ON MY OWN I FEEL KIND OF
    BLUE
NOTHING I'D RATHER DO THAN DANCE WITH YOU
    WO YEH
SEE THE BOYS ROCKIN'
DO THE BOYS ROCK, DO THE BOYS ROCK AND
    ROLL?

Chorus:
DO THE BOYS ROCK YEH YEH
DO THE BOYS ROLL YEH YEH
DO THE BOYS ROCK YEH YEH
DO THE BOYS ROLL YEH YEH
DO THE BOYS ROCK, DO THE BOYS ROCK AND
    ROLL

Verse 5:
WELL I'M THIRTY FIVE AND I'M STILL ALIVE
I GOT ARTHRITIS BUT I STILL DO THE JIVE OH
    YEH
REELIN' AND A ROCKIN'
DO THE BOYS ROCK, DO THE BOYS ROCK AND
    ROLL.

Verse 6:
GONNA PACK MY THINGS AND GO HELL BOUND
THIS HEARTBREAK HOTEL GETS ME DOWN WO
    YEH
REELIN' AND A ROCKIN'
DO THE BOYS ROCK, DO THE BOYS ROCK AN'
    ROLL.

Chorus:
DO THE BOYS ROCK YEH YEH
DO THE BOYS ROLL YEH YEH
DO THE BOYS ROCK YEH YEH
DO THE BOYS ROLL YEH YEH
DO THE BOYS ROCK, DO THE BOYS ROCK AND
    ROLL

VOICE OFF: What's all this noise going on in 'ere?

(General booing)

BOYS: Oh, not again . . . Shut up . . . (Etc.)

(The shadow appears again - then SQUEERS enters at the top of stairs)

SQUEERS: *(leaning over stairs)* What's all this noise, I say?

GRAYMARSH: *(who has his back to the stairs, still thinking this is another of the boys mimicking Squeers)* Oh, shut up!

(He turns and sees SQUEERS who slowly comes down the stairs and over to GRAYMARSH. The other BOYS back away leaving GRAYMARSH on his own. SQUEERS threatens GRAYMARSH who retreats. SQUEERS lashes out at GRAYMARSH who catches it across the face)

SQUEERS: Get away.

(The BOYS slowly form into lines)

(To NICHOLAS) Here's a fine thing, the pump's froze.

NICHOLAS: *(absent mindedly)* Indeed.

SQUEERS: Ay, so you can't wash yourself this morning.

NICHOLAS: Not wash myself?

SQUEERS: No. Not a bit of you. So you must be content with giving yourself a dry polish till we can break the ice in the well and get a bucketful out for the boys. Don't stand there staring at me, but look sharp will you.

(NICHOLAS puts on his jacket)

(MRS. SQUEERS enters with FANNY at the top of the stairs, bearing triumphantly the bottle of Brimstone)

Ah! Come in my love. It's Brimstone morning. We purify the boys blood now and then, Nickleby.

MRS. SQUEERS: Purify fiddlesticks ends. Don't think, young man, that we go to the expense of flower of brimstone and molasses just to purify them; because if you think we carry on the business in that way, you'll find yourself mistaken, and so I tell you plainly.

SQUEERS: *(frowning)* My dear, Hem!

MRS. SQUEERS: Oh! nonsense. If the young man comes to be a teacher here let him understand at once that we don't want any foolery about the boys. They have the brimstone and treacle, partly because if they hadn't something or other in the way of medicine they'd be always ailing and giving a world of trouble, and partly because it spoils their appetites and comes cheaper than breakfast and dinner. So it does them good and us good at the same time, and that's fair enough, I'm sure. Fanny, the spoon.

FANNY: The spoon? Haven't you got it?

MRS. SQUEERS: I thought you had it.

TOGETHER: Who's got the spoon?

(As the music to BRIMSTONE & TREACLE begins MRS. SQUEERS and FANNY search furiously for the spoon. In fact one of the boys had it and they now pass it mischievously along the line. Their backs are turned to the Audience at this stage and we can see the spoon changing from one hand to another. Eventually MRS. SQUEERS realizes what is going on, she pushes one boy out of the line, and taking his place grabs the spoon as it reaches her)

Song: BRIMSTONE AND TREACLE"

MRS. SQUEERS: FIFTY BOYS AT TWENTY POUNDS A YEAR
FEEDING THEM AIN'T EASY
OH YOU'VE NO IDEA.
COST PER HEAD FOR SUPPLYING FOOD
IS SEVEN PENCE A WEEK
AND THEN THERE'S MR. SQUEERS.
SO I'VE FOUND A SYSTEM
OF REDUCING THE DEMAND
START THE DAY WITH THINGS THAT
MAKE THEIR HUNGER DISAPPEAR.

BRIMSTONE AND TREACLE.
GOOD FOR YOUNG PEOPLE.
HELPS TO KEEP THEIR APPETITES AT BAY.
BRIMSTONE AND TREACLE.
SUCH A FINE MEAL
KEEPS YOU FULL TO THE END OF THE DAY.
THEY'RE LIVING IN GOOD HEALTH
AND GIVING US OUR WEALTH.
THAT'S THE WAY WE WORK IT IN THIS HALL.

BOYS:
FIFTY BOYS AT TWENTY POUNDS A YEAR.
FEEDING US AIN'T EASY
OH YOU'VE NO IDEA.
COST PER HEAD FOR SUPPLYING FOOD
IS SEVEN PENCE A WEEK
AND THEN THERE'S MR. SQUEERS.
SO SHE'S FOUND A SYSTEM
OF REDUCING THE DEMAND
START THE DAY WITH THINGS THAT MAKE
OUR HUNGER DISAPPEAR.

BRIMSTONE AND TREACLE.
GOOD FOR YOUNG PEOPLE.
HELPS TO KEEP OUR APPETITES AT BAY.
BRIMSTONE AND TREACLE
SUCH A FINE MEAL.
KEEPS US FULL TO THE END OF THE DAY.

MRS. SQUEERS:
THE POTION MAY BE FOUL
BUT IT PURIFIES THE BOWEL.
THAT'S THE WAY WE WORK IT IN THIS HALL.

BOYS:
BRIMSTONE AND TREACLE,
La La La La La,
GOOD FOR YOUNG PEOPLE
La La etc . . .
BRIMSTONE AND TREACLE
La La La La La,
SUCH A FINE MEAL,
La La etc . . .
BRIMSTONE AND TREACLE
TIME TODAY

SQUEERS:
Now to business. Let any boy speak a word without leave and I'll take the skin off his back. *(Addresses the assembled BOYS pompously)* Boys, I've been to London and have returned to my family, and you, as strong and well as ever.

(The BOYS give feeble cheers)

I've seen the parents of some boys and they're so glad to hear how their sons are getting on, that there's no prospect at all of their going away, which of course is a very pleasant thing to reflect upon, for all parties. I've had disappointments to contend against. Bolder's father was two pound ten short. Where is Bolder?

BOYS:
Here he is, please sir. *(Pointing at cowering youth)*

SQUEERS:
Come 'ere, Bolder. Bolder *(Picks boy up by the ear)* We don't like little boys whose parents don't pay.

BOLDER:
Please sir, it's not my fault.

SQUEERS:	Silence, you incorrigible young scoundrel *(Cuffs him a-round the ear)* and as the last thrashing did you no good we must see what another will do. *(Beats the boy)* Put him out Smike -

(SMIKE leads BOLDER out - returns to take up his previous position)

A letter for Cobbey. Stand up Cobbey! *(Reads letter)* Oh! Cobbey's mother's dead and his Uncle John has took to drinkin; which is all his sister sends, except eighteen pence which will just pay for that broken square of glass. Mrs. Squeers, my dear, will you take the money?

(MRS. SQUEERS pockets money in businesslike manner)

MRS. SQUEERS:	Graymarsh, he's the next, stand Graymarsh!

(GRAYMARSH stands up)

SQUEERS:	Graymarsh's stepmother took to her bed on hearing that he wouldn't eat fat and has been very ill ever since. She wishes to know, by an early post, where he expects to go if he quarrels with his victuals; and with what feelings he could turn up his nose at the cow's liver broth after his good master had asked a blessing on it. She is sorry to find he is discontented, which is sinful and horrid and hopes Mr. Squeers will flog him into a happier state of mind; with this view she has also stopped his ha'penny a week pocket money and given double-bladed knife with a corkscrew in it to the missionaries, which she had bought on purpose for him.

(Hands 'letter' to MRS. SQUEERS, who holds up blank sheet of paper to Audience, grimaces, scratches and shakes head)

A sulky state of feeling won't do. Cheerfulness and contentment must be kept up. Graymarsh come 'ere boy! *(Beats GRAYMARSH)* That'll learn you to quarrel with your victuals.

Now Nickleby. Take the boys outside, break the ice in the well, and wash them down before they come back for classes. *(To the BOYS)* Look sharp will you?

NICHOLAS:	*(in a gentler tone than Squeers')* Now boys. *(He ushers them out)*

(Exit all except SQUEERS, MRS. SQUEERS and FANNY)

MRS. SQUEERS:	*(mimicking)* Now boys! Follow your leader boys. Ooh that Knuckleboy. I hate him.
SQUEERS:	What do you hate him for my dear?

MRS. SQUEERS: What's that to you? If I hate him, that's enough ain't it?

SQUEERS: Quite enough for him my dear, and a great deal too much I daresay, if he knew it. I only asked from curiosity my dear.

MRS. SQUEERS: Well then, if you want to know, I'll tell you. Because he's a proud, haughty, consequential, turned-up nosed peacock!

SQUEERS: Hem! He is cheap my dear, the young man is very cheap.

MRS. SQUEERS: Not a bit of it.

SQUEERS: Five pound a year.

MRS. SQUEERS: What of that? It's dear if you don't want him isn't it?

SQUEERS: But we DO want him.

MRS. SQUEERS: I don't see that you want him any more than the dead. Don't tell me. You can put on the cards and in the advertisements "Education by Mr. Wackford Squeers and able assistants", without having any assistants, can't you? I've no patience with you.

SQUEERS: *(sternly)* Haven't you! Now I'll tell you what, Mrs. Squeers. In this matter of having a teacher I'll take my own way, if you please. A slave-driver in the West Indies is allowed a man under him, to see that his blacks don't run away or get up a rebellion; and I'll have a man under me, to do the same with OUR blacks till such time as little Wackford is able to take charge of the school.

MRS. SQUEERS: He's a nasty stuck up monkey, that's what I consider of that Knuckleboy.

FANNY: Where did you find this Knuckleboy, Father?

SQUEERS: NICKLEBY. Your mother always calls things and people by their wrong names.

MRS. SQUEERS: No matter for that. I see them with right eyes, and that's quite enough for me. I watched him when you were laying on to little Bolder just now. He looked as black as thunder all the while, and one time started up as if he had more than got it in his mind to make a rush at you. I saw him, though he thought I didn't.

(Before SQUEERS can reply)

FANNY: Never mind that Father. Who is the man?

MRS. SQUEERS: Why, your father has got some nonsense in his head that he's the son of a poor gentleman that died the other day.

FANNY: The son of a gentleman!

MRS. SQUEERS: Yes, but I don't believe a word of it.

SQUEERS: Whatever he is my dear, we make a very good friend by having him here; and if he likes to learn the boys anything besides minding them, I have no objection, I am sure.

MRS. SQUEERS: *(vehemently)* I say again, I hate him worse than poison.

(Change of lighting)

(6 notes of the "SMIKE" theme to evoke change of atmosphere)

(One spotlight falls on MRS. SQUEERS)

(NICHOLAS enters. Another spotlight falls on him)

(SQUEERS and FANNY freeze)

(MRS. SQUEERS moves very slowly towards NICHOLAS, and beckons him to join her. As they go upstage the two spots merge into one. MRS. SQUEERS leads NICHOLAS to a couch which in the darkness has been placed upstage. During this following fantasy sequence MRS. SQUEERS' voice takes on a less coarse and more seductive air. SQUEERS and FANNY exit unnoticed in darkness)

Come and sit down here with me. Have you ever had your fortune told?

(In front of the couch there is also a small round table on which there is a pack of cards. MRS. SQUEERS picks them up)

If you want to know the truth about your future, listen carefully, and I will reveal all.

Song: "YOUR KIND OF WOMAN"

MRS. SQUEERS: TAKE THESE CARDS AND PUT THEM DOWN
TURNED UP IN ROWS OF THREE.
TWELVE'S ENOUGH FOR NOW YOUNG MAN,
SO TELL ME WHAT YOU SEE.

NICHOLAS: IT SEEMS I'VE GOT THE KNAVE OF HEARTS
AND ALL THE KINGS AND QUEENS.
AND HERE'S THE EIGHT OF DIAMONDS . . .

MRS. SQUEERS: AH I'LL TELL YOU WHAT THIS MEANS!
THE QUEEN OF HEARTS INFORMS ME
THERE'S A WOMAN IN YOUR LIFE
THE KING OF SPADES SUGGESTS
IT COULD BE SOMEONE ELSE'S WIFE.

NICHOLAS: BUT THIS IS QUITE ABSURD
BECAUSE I CANNOT THINK OF WHO

MRS. SQUEERS: WELL HERE'S THE NINE OF HEARTS
WHICH SHOWS THAT THIS WILL ALL COME TRUE.

(MRS. SQUEERS sidles up to NICHOLAS on the couch)

SHE COULD BE YOUR KIND OF WOMAN
TAKE HER, HOLD HER
AND NEVER SCOLD HER
WHEN SHE TELLS YOU SHE NEEDS YOUR LOVING.
SHE COULD BE YOUR KIND OF WOMAN
AND YOU COULD BE HER KIND OF MAN.

NICHOLAS: MA'AM I DO DECLARE
THERE IS A JOKER IN THE PACK.
I WON'T BE TAKEN IN
AS EASILY AS THAT

MRS. SQUEERS: BUT EVERYTHING MAKES SENSE,
YOU ARE THE KNAVE OF HEARTS YOU SEE
THE DIAMOND EIGHT PROPOSES
THAT THE QUEEN OF HEARTS IS ME.

SPEAKS: YOU MAY LOOK AT ME
AND THINK I'M NOT YOUR CUP OF TEA
APPEARANCES HOWEVER
CAN FROM TIME TO TIME DECEIVE
AND AGE CAN BE AN ASSET
THOUGH I'M NOT AS OLD AS THAT,
IN FACT YOUNG MAN I'M ONLY THIRTY-THREE.

(Set transforms into a sleazy "Strip" joint)

I COULD BE YOUR KIND OF WOMAN
TAKE ME, HOLD ME
AND NEVER SCOLD ME
WHEN I TELL YOU I NEED YOUR LOVING
I COULD BE YOUR KIND OF WOMAN
AND YOU COULD BE MY KIND OF MAN.

I COULD BE YOUR KIND OF WOMAN
AND YOU COULD BE MY KIND OF MAN,
I GOT TO TELL YOU
YOU COULD BE MY KIND OF MAN.
I'LL SAY IT ONCE MORE
YOU COULD BE MY KIND OF MAN.

(MRS. SQUEERS stands up and goes into a "strip" routine with lights flashing)

(During the instrumental break FANNY and TILDA enter and join in the "strip" routine)

(At the end of this number MRS. SQUEERS finds herself at the same spot as when the fantasy sequence began. The lighting returns to the one spot on her. In the surrounding darkness SQUEERS and FANNY return to their frozen postures and only come to life again when full lighting is restored)

MRS. SQUEERS: *(vehemently)* I say again, I hate him worse than poison.

SQUEERS: If you dislike him, my dear, I don't know anybody who can show dislike better than you, and of course there's no occasion, with him, to take the trouble to hide your feelings.

MRS. SQUEERS: I don't intend to, I assure you.

SQUEERS: That's right. And if he has a touch of pride about him, as I think he has, I don't believe there's a woman in all England that can bring anybody's spirit down as quick as you can, my love.

(MRS. SQUEERS chuckles. NICHOLAS enters in exactly the same way as he did in the fantasy sequence, except that this time the lighting stays up. Slight pause as MRS. SQUEERS looks at NICHOLAS. NICHOLAS ushers the BOYS in)

SQUEERS: Right boys. Time for lessons. Sit down. *(He hurries them along swishing his cane in the air)* This is the first class in English, Spelling and Philosophy, Nickleby. *(Beckons NICHOLAS to his side)* Now then, first boy, where is he?

BOY: Please sir, he's cleaning down the back parlour window.

SQUEERS: So he is to be sure. We go upon the practical mode of teaching Nickleby; the regular education system. C-L-E-A-N clean, verb, active, to make bright, to scour. W-I-N win, D-E-R der, winder, a casement. When a boy knows this out of a book, he goes and does it. Where's the second boy?

2ND BOY: Please sir, he's weeding the garden.

SQUEERS: To be sure, so he is. B-O-T bot, T-I-N tin, bottin, N-E-Y ney, bottiney. When he has learnt that bottiney means a knowledge of plants, he has to get to know 'em. Third boy, what is a horse?

BOLDER: A beast, sir.

SQUEERS: So it is, ain't it, Nickleby?

NICHOLAS: I believe there is no doubt of that, sir.

SQUEERS: Of course there isn't. A horse is a quadruped and quadruped's Latin for beast, as everyone that's been through grammar knows, or else what's the use of having grammars at all?

NICHOLAS: (abstractly) What indeed.

SQUEERS: (to BOLDER) As you're perfect in that, go and look after my horse and see he gets something to eat . . .

(BOLDER exits)

. . . That's our system, Nickleby, what do you think of it?

NICHOLAS: (sarcastically) It's a very useful one at any rate.

SQUEERS: Good, good, then I can leave you to take the Latin class while I er . . . stretch my legs. (He exits Left)

(Without SQUEERS noticing some boys tip their hands backwards and forwards knowingly, indicating that in fact SQUEERS is going for a drink)

NICHOLAS: Do you have Latin books?

BOYS: Yes sir. (They take them out)

NICHOLAS: Not very many copies are there? Just do the best you can and share. Pay attention now, all together. Decline AMO.

BOYS: AMO, AMAS, AMAT, AMAMUS, AMATIS, AMANT.

NICHOLAS: Now BELLUM.

BOYS: BELLUM, BELLUM, BELLUM, BELLI, BELLO, BELLO, BELLA, BELLA, BELLA, BELLORUM, BELLIS, BELLIS.

NICHOLAS: Once again.

BOYS: BELLA, BELLA, BELLA, BLA, BLA, BLA, BLA, BLA.

(Their voices fade as lights pick out FANNY and TILDA who have just entered and are looking over at NICHOLAS)

TILDA: Fancy dragging me all this way, I should be helping my man.

FANNY: *(points to NICHOLAS)* Tilda it's worth it. Look! The
                man I shall marry!

TILDA: Has he asked you already, then?

FANNY: Well, not asked, but he's made his intentions very clear.

TILDA: You've been dreaming, my girl, if you think that he loves
                you.

FANNY: *(ignores her and goes into a swoon)* I made a great im-
                pression on him at dinner. I don't think he ever met any-
                one like me before.

TILDA: I should say so.

FANNY: Ah, you're only jealous, I'll show you.

*(She moves down the steps. Lights fade except on FANNY and TILDA.
A small spot comes up on NICHOLAS)*

(MUSIC - 6 notes of the "SMIKE" theme)

*(TILDA goes into a dream trance and just watches. NICHOLAS is still
reading from his Latin book, but in mime)*

FANNY: *(ECHO on voice)* Nicholas . . .

*(She has changed from the girl we know. All is slow motion and ultra
dream like. NICHOLAS turns to FANNY, puts down his book and opens his
arms)*

NICHOLAS: I love you.

Song: "WE'LL FIND OUR DAY"

(Set transforms to church with stained glass windows)

*(In this fantasy sequence any exaggerated ballet movements should be
used. The BOYS could enter dressed as choirboys, and sing the harmonies to
"We'll find our day.")*

                Song: "WE'LL FIND OUR DAY"

NICHOLAS: YOU AND I
                WE'LL TOUCH THE SKY.
                REACH OUT AND COME TO ME
                AND TEACH ME HOW TO FLY.

FANNY: I LOVE YOU,
                I NEED YOU,
                I BELIEVE YOU WHEN YOU SAY.

BOTH: WE'LL FIND OUR DAY.
                WE'LL FIND OUR DAY.
                WE'LL FIND OUR DAY.

FANNY: YOU BELONG
                TO MY LOVE SONG.
                I'VE FOUND THE TUNE
                AND I LIKE SINGING YOU.

NICHOLAS: I LOVE YOU,
                I NEED YOU,
                I BELIEVE YOU WHEN YOU SAY.

BOTH: WE'LL FIND OUR DAY.
                WE'LL FIND OUR DAY.
                WE'LL FIND OUR DAY.

(The song finishes and FANNY goes over to TILDA. NICHOLAS picks up his book and continues his lesson. Lights up on TILDA who comes back to life)

TILDA: Get on with you, go and talk to him.

FANNY: *(furious)* I'll show you. *(She rushes in)*

(Lights C & R return)

                Beg your pardon, I thought my father was or might be . . . how very awkward.

NICHOLAS: Mr. Squeers is out.

FANNY: Do you know how long he will be?

NICHOLAS: I've no idea, Miss Squeers.

FANNY: Oh . . . please as a kindness, call me Fanny. *(She leers at him . . . pause . . . she gives a forced laugh)* Sorry I disturbed you.

(She backs out. She turns to TILDA who urges her back. She turns back to NICHOLAS who is once more facing the class. She clears her throat)

                Ah, Mr. Nickleby.

NICHOLAS: *(slightly laconically, since he finds the continued disturbance irritating)* Yes.

FANNY: If I hadn't thought my father was here, I wouldn't have disturbed you. I was looking for a . . . um . . . a pen.

NICHOLAS: If that's all you want can I help? Shall it be a hard or a soft nib?

FANNY: *(behind her hand to TILDA)* Ooh, he has a beautiful smile.

NICHOLAS: Which did you say?

FANNY: Dear me, I was thinking of something else for a moment, I do declare. As hard as possible, if you please.

(She sighs a very theatrical, sigh, with her hand on her throat, it has no effect on NICHOLAS, he is busy cutting her nib. He gives it to her and she drops it. They both stoop to pick it up and knock heads)
(The class laughs)

NICHOLAS: Very awkward of me.

FANNY: Not at all, sir, it was my fault.

(They look at each other. NICHOLAS is obviously embarrassed and hands FANNY the nib)

NICHOLAS: Was there anything else?

FANNY: Er . . . no, I don't think so, thank you.

NICHOLAS: Well can I return to my lesson?

FANNY: Oh, please don't let me stop you. *(She stands and looks at him with a vacant stare)*

NICHOLAS: I'm waiting for you to leave, so I may carry on.

TILDA: *(from the platform)* Really, Mr. Nickleby, I wouldn't have thought you'd have minded your young lady standing in while you work.

(FANNY gives TILDA a foul look. The BOYS titter)

NICHOLAS: *(covered in confusion)* I assure you madam, the relationship that you suggest between Miss Squeers and myself, is completely unfounded.

TILDA: Oh, I made a great impression on him at dinner . . . he'd never met anyone like me before . . . *(She titters)*

FANNY: *(fish-wife)* Matilda Price . . . you . . . you interfering old busy-body. This affair is no concern of yours.

(Turns her back on TILDA and smiles sweetly at NICHOLAS. The smile fades as TILDA says)

TILDA: Huh! This affair is no concern of yours. And Mr. Nickleby ain't much interested in it neither.

FANNY: *(stretching round)* You little tartar, just you wait till I get my hands on your ugly mouth. You're nothing but a . . . . a . . . a.

NICHOLAS: Er, yes, well. I think it's time for a break now boys, come along. Excuse us LADIES.

(He shepherds the BOYS off. They use every exit possible)

FANNY: *(starts picking up books and flinging them at TILDA, who retreats)* Get out of my sight. I never want to see you again. Get out. Get out. I hate you, I hate you, I hate you.

(FANNY begins to cry tears of rage. TILDA exits on her line)

TILDA: You listen to me Fanny Squeers. It'll be a mighty fine cold day before you catch a man like Mr. Nickleby. *(She stamps off up the stairs)*

(FANNY runs riot)

FANNY: Get out!!! *(She flings a book at TILDA)*

(There is absolute chaos, as she throws and rips books, snaps rulers etc. her rage slowly subsides. She stops and looks at the mess she has created, then stoops to begin to tidy up. She then stands again and once more looks at the mess)

(to herself) Look at my dress. *(Calling loud)* Smike . . . Smike . . . Smike.

(SMIKE enters and looks around at the mess)

Smike, clear this mess up - and if it's not tidy by the time I come back, I'll tell my father. *(She exits)*

(SMIKE looks at the chaos, his shoulders sag and he methodically begins to tidy up. He has only just begun when SQUEERS enters at the top of the stairs. He comes down to the platform)

SQUEERS: Where's Mr. Nickleby?

(He sees the mess and stops dead, he then sees SMIKE who appears from behind a desk he has been tidying. SQUEERS makes for SMIKE)

Ruined. My books, my precious books, ruined. Smike, come 'ere.

SMIKE: I . . . it wasn't . . . it wasn't me, sir.

SQUEERS: So you deny it would you - you've always hated me. Me, who's been like a father to you all these years.

SMIKE: Please sir . . .

SQUEERS: So that's your way of paying me back for all my kindness.

SMIKE: No, sir.

SQUEERS: Oh, so you don't feel any gratitude. *(He grabs SMIKE and almost lifts him from the ground.)* This time you snivelling little rat, you've gone too far. I'm going to teach you a lesson in front of all the others. *(He drags SMIKE to the stairs and calls)* Mr. Nickleby, be so good as to bring the boys in here.

(He throws SMIKE across the room and stands over him, rolling up his sleeves. NICHOLAS and BOYS enter. They come on from the stairs and D. R. and D.L. and from behind black masking flats)

Let this be a lesson to all boys who would not show gratitude. Is every boy here?

(MRS. SQUEERS enters with FANNY and WACKFORD. MRS. SQUEERS comes down in front of the master's desk. FANNY stands on the stairs)

Mr. Nickleby, to your desk.

NICHOLAS: What is going on?

SQUEERS: This spiteful little boy has destroyed all the books.

NICHOLAS: Is this possible, sir? Have the goodness to consider . . .

SQUEERS: None of your whining, vapouring here, Master puppy. Be off to your kennel. *(He points to the desk. Turns to SMIKE)* Stand a little out of the way Mrs. Squeers, my dear. I've hardly got enough room.

SMIKE: Spare me, sir.

SQUEERS: Oh, that's all is it? Yes, I'll flog you within an inch of your life, and I'll spare you that.

MRS. SQUEERS: Ha, ha, ha! That's a good 'un!

SMIKE: I was told to clear up the mess.

SQUEERS: Trying to put the blame on somebody else are you? You nasty, ungrateful, pig headed, brutish, obstinate, sneaking dog.

(He knocks SMIKE's head with every syllable. He prepares to strike SMIKE with a cane)

NICHOLAS: STOP!!

SQUEERS: *(freezes)* Who cried stop? *(Savagely)*

NICHOLAS: I did, Squeers. This must not go on.

SQUEERS: Must not go on? *(He releases SMIKE and turns to confront NICHOLAS)*

NICHOLAS: I say, must not. And, shall not, I will prevent it.

   Song: "HERE I AM"

(NICHOLAS pulls SMIKE away from SQUEERS and faces MR. and MRS. SQUEERS threateningly)

NICHOLAS: YOU ASK ME WHAT EVERYTHING'S ABOUT
           AND WHAT ON EARTH I'M DOING HERE.
           I'VE NEWS FOR YOU, I'VE UNDERSTOOD,
           HE MADE THE ANSWER CLEAR!
           SO HERE I AM
           AND NICKLEBY'S MY NAME!
           UNDERSTAND.
           THAT REVOLUTION IS MY GAME.
           STICK AROUND, YOU WILL HAVE FOUND
           THIS PLACE WILL NEVER BE THE SAME AGAIN.

BOYS: NICKLEBY, WHO WANTS US TO BE FREE,
           HE'S GOING TO BE, A REVOLUTIONARY.
           STICK AROUND, YOU WILL HAVE FOUND
           THIS PLACE WILL NEVER BE THE SAME AGAIN.

NICHOLAS: IF YOU THINK YOU'VE GOT A BETTER SONG
                              THAN ME
           THEN GO AHEAD AND SING.
           AT LEAST THE TUNE I'M CALLING NOW
           HAS GOT THEM FOLLOWING.

(BOYS advance upon SQUEERS' family who retreat nervously)

BOYS: NICKLEBY, WHO WANTS US TO BE FREE
HE'S GONNA BE, A REVOLUTIONARY.
STICK AROUND, YOU WILL HAVE FOUND
THIS PLACE WILL NEVER BE THE SAME AGAIN.
Da Da etc . . . . .

NICHOLAS: IF YOU THINK YOU'VE GOT A BETTER SONG
THAN ME
THEN GO AHEAD AND SING.
AT LEAST THE TUNE I'M CALLING NOW
HAS GOT THEM FOLLOWING.

BOYS: NICKLEBY, WHO WANTS US TO BE FREE
HE'S GONNA BE, A REVOLUTIONARY.
STICK AROUND, YOU WILL HAVE FOUND
THIS PLACE WILL NEVER BE THE SAME AGAIN.

Da da da da da da da da da etc . . .
. . . . WE'RE FREE.

(During the number the BOYS run riot and overpower the SQUEERS family. Books are thrown, desks are upturned, the furniture is wrecked. MRS. SQUEERS is forced to take large doses of brimstone, WACKFORD JUNIOR'S head is immersed in the brimstone bowl, FANNY is surrounded by screaming boys. Eventually the SQUEERS family is driven out, some of the boys chase after them triumphantly. Crescendo of noise is followed by sudden silence and blackout)

TRANSITION

Music. "SMIKE" THEME SONG is played on one instrument.

ACT TWO

Scene Two

MODERN SCHOOL

Very slowly the lights come up again. There is chaos everywhere. The background set has changed back to the modern school. The chaos of Dotheboys Hall has been transformed to chaos in the classroom. Books, papers everywhere.

BOYS (in modern costume) drift on in ones and twos and survey the scene.

TUBBY: Blimey, what's been going on in here? Now we'll be in trouble.

BROWN: He's right you know. It does look like the battle of Waterloo.

COATES: Who tore my book up?

MARSH: Don't you remember? That was me, just before we pushed Squeersy in the corner.

PLANK: Somebody's trodden on my pen.

BROWN: That's alright. Now you can't do any more written work.

PLANK: Oh yes. You try explaining that to my dad. He'll make me buy a new one, I expect.

COATES: We'll never get this lot cleared up.

TUBBY: It'll takes ages.

SMEETON: No it won't. If we all lend a hand, we could clear it up in no time. Give me a hand with this desk. Why don't we change it round a bit? . . . Like that . . .

(New arrangement of desks is now less formal, with the teacher's desk integrated in the middle of the pupils)
(The new arrangement is in a semicircle)

That's better. Now we'll be able to see each other.

BROWN: You're very happy all of a sudden.

MARSH: Must have been the musical.

SMEETON: How do you mean?

MARSH:	You playing the part of Smike at Dotheboys Hall. Aren't you glad it wasn't for real?
SMEETON:	Well of course it wasn't real.
MARSH:	I know, but for a while it was though, wasn't it?
SMEETON:	I suppose so, except that . . . well it's funny, I can remember being here *(He stands thoughtfully and points to a spot downstage)* and then Squeers came along, and we started to sing and dance. But it felt like I was dreaming.
COATES:	I know what you mean. Now it's over, it makes you wonder if it all really happened.
TUBBY:	Of course it did. Mr. Nicholls was Nicholas Nickleby and Miss Grant was Fanny.
BROWN:	And I was Bolder, can't you remember?
SMEETON:	Yes of course I can. But . . .
MARSH:	You know the bit when Nickleby was talking to you. You sounded really fed up.
SMEETON:	I was. Yes, I suppose I was. But things got better for a while.
TUBBY:	And I was Wackford.
BROWN:	And Coates was Cobbey.
MARSH:	And I was Greymarsh.
COATES:	And then there was Mrs. Squeers.
BROWN:	Yes, she was played by . . . *(He hesitates)*
PLANK:	She was . . . *(He looks very puzzled)*
SMEETON:	See what I mean.
BROWN:	Well I can remember her perfectly well. I'll never forget her.

(MISS GRANT enters U.R.)

MISS GRANT:	Good gracious, what has been going on in here?

(PLANK looks at her with a puzzled look. He just seems to be getting somewhere but the glimmer fades. He shrugs his shoulders)

MARSH:	We've been doing Nicholas Nickleby, Miss Grant.

MISS GRANT: I see. Well I think the headmaster had better know what you've been up to. *(She exits)*

BROWN: Do you know, I've got a feeling . . .

SMEETON: Yes, I know what you mean. I'm sure it must have happened really.

(Starts to hum "Don't let life get you down")

I can remember. I'm sure that's why I'm so happy.

(SMEETON leads the BOYS into:

Reprise: "DON'T LET LIFE GET YOU DOWN")

(Then

Reprise: "IN THE WARM LIGHT OF A BRAND NEW DAY")

Reprise: "DON'T LET LIFE GET YOU DOWN"

SMEETON: PEOPLE THINK THEY SEE A MOUNTAIN,
BUT IT'S JUST A LITTLE HILL,
AND THE PROBLEMS THAT SURROUND THEM
ARE JUST THE MOOD THEY FEEL,
BUT DANGERS IN THE DARKNESS ARE ONLY
                IN THE MIND.

Chorus: DON'T LET LIFE GET YOU DOWN.
EVEN THOUGH THE WORLD MIGHT LET YOU
              DOWN.
COS DANGERS IN THE DARKNESS
ARE ONLY IN YOUR MIND
BETTER KEEP YOUR EYES WIDE OPEN, LOOK
              AROUND.
DON'T LET LIFE GET YOU DOWN
EVEN THOUGH THE WORLD MIGHT LET YOU
              DOWN.
DON'T LET LIFE
DON'T LET LIFE
DON'T LET LIFE GET YOU DOWN.

Reprise: "IN THE WARM LIGHT OF A
BRAND NEW DAY"

SMEETON: I FOUND A LONG LOST HAPPINESS
WHEN I WOKE UP TODAY
THE COLD I FELT INSIDE OF ME
CAN NOW BE PUSHED AWAY.
COS WHEN I'M FEELING LOST
I'LL KEEP MY FINGERS CROSSED
AND TRY TO SHOW THAT I DON'T CARE
IN THE WARM LIGHT OF A BRAND NEW DAY . . .

(HEADMASTER enters D.R. with MISS GRANT)

HEADMASTER: It doesn't look too bad, Miss Grant.

MISS GRANT: Well, I . . . I thought . . .

SMEETON: Do you like our new arrangements, sir? Or do you want us to put it back as it was before?

HEADMASTER: As it was before? Oh no, leave it as it is. Less of a barrier between you and me like this, isn't it? I've been going through Nicholas Nickleby.

BROWN: So have we sir.

HEADMASTER: Quite. It's a frightening book you know. *(He holds the book in the air)* . . . Particularly the end. Mr. Squeers got what was coming to him. Should have realised that you can't hold fifty boys down for very long. They finally got the better of him. *(to SMEETON)* And how are you feeling?

SMEETON: Very well, thank you sir.

HEADMASTER: Good. *(He takes SMEETON aside)* I've just received a letter from your foster parents. They think we should all get together and have a little chat about your future. But I'll speak to you about that later.

SMEETON: *(rather bewildered)* Yes sir.

HEADMASTER: *(turns back to class)* Now, about putting Nicholas Nickleby to music. D'you know, I think we could all learn something from it.

PLANK: But sir . . . We've already . . .

HEADMASTER: You probably don't realize that there would be a lot of problems. Costumes, make-up, sets, lighting and so on. But I'm quite sure Miss Grant and Mr. Nicholls will manage.

COATES: But we've already done it, sir.

HEADMASTER: When?

COATES: Just now.

HEADMASTER: Oh I see, on your own you mean. That was probably all the mess you know, Miss Grant.

(MISS GRANT laughs)

You can't put on a show just like that, you know. Can they, Miss Grant?

MISS GRANT: Good gracious me no. It takes weeks of study.

HEADMASTER: Yes there's plenty of preparation to be done. Rehearsals are going to take up a lot of our time.

BROWN: Do you mean we'd have to practise in class time, sir?

HEADMASTER: I think we shall have to, don't you, Miss Grant?

MISS GRANT: Well I'm sure you'll be able to change the class periods around, Headmaster.

HEADMASTER: You're right. We'll never be able to get it done otherwise.

COATES: You mean we'd be able to do acting instead of reading and writing all the time?

HEADMASTER: Yes, and besides, you'd get to know Nicholas Nickleby very well if you've learnt all the lines.

PLANK: But we already know Nicholas Nickl . . .

(He is silenced by BROWN who places a hand over his mouth)

BROWN: It would be a most enjoyable way of studying the book, wouldn't it, sir?

TUBBY: Learning by doing's much more fun.

BROWN: *(mimicking SQUEERS' voice)* We'd go upon the practical mode of teaching.

(There is a pause)

SMEETON: Would you play the part of the Headmaster, like we agreed, sir?

HEADMASTER: Yes.

BROWN: And could we put it on at the end of term, sir?

HEADMASTER: Yes.

SMEETON: Instead of the breaking up assembly?

HEADMASTER: The breaking up assembly? *(He laughs)* Well that might be a good thing.

SMEETON: Could we rehearse every day?

HEADMASTER: Yes.

SMEETON: Instead of the daily test?

HEADMASTER: Well . . . Yes alright.

(The class cheer and gather round the HEADMASTER and MISS GRANT, talking about the parts they want to play)

(Lights fade on everyone. Except on NICHOLLS who enters and walks forwards away from the excited but silent group of BOYS)

(Low mellow lighting)

Song: "BELIEVE"

Song: "BELIEVE"

NICHOLLS: YOU THOUGHT THAT WE WERE ALWAYS ACTING,
                  YOU SAID THAT WE WERE INSINCERE,
                  BUT NOW OUR PLAY IS DONE,
                  AND NOW OUR LIFE'S BEGUN.

Chorus: BELIEVE, BELIEVE IN WHAT I'M SAYING
                  HOW THE WORLD'S A STAGE
                  BELIEVE, BELIEVE IN WHAT I TELL YOU
                  NOW THE FEELING'S CHANGED.

NICHOLLS: ALL THE LINES I LEARNT HAVE LEFT ME
                  EVERYTHING I SAY I FEEL,
                  THE WORLD OF MAKE BELIEVING
                  WE'LL LEAVE BEHIND FOR REAL.

NICHOLLS & BOYS:	Chorus: BELIEVE, BELIEVE IN WHAT I'M SAYING
NICHOLLS:	HOW THE WORLD'S A STAGE
NICHOLLS & BOYS:	BELIEVE, BELIEVE IN WHAT I TELL YOU NOW THE FEELING'S CHANGED.
NICHOLLS:	THE ACTOR'S SMILE HAS TURNED TO FROWNING, THEY'VE BROUGHT THE FINAL CURTAIN DOWN. THEY'VE TURNED THE LIGHTS DOWN LOW. THE PEOPLE START TO GO.
NICHOLLS & BOYS:	Chorus: BELIEVE, BELIEVE IN WHAT I'M SAYING
NICHOLLS:	HOW THE WORLD'S A STAGE
NICHOLLS & BOYS:	BELIEVE, BELIEVE IN WHAT I TELL YOU
NICHOLLS:	NOW THE FEELING'S CHANGED

Repeat BELIEVE chorus twice.

Song ends.

(At the end of BELIEVE which everyone is singing CURTAIN falls)

(CURTAIN CALL)

(2 choruses of DOTHEBOYS ROCK followed by instrumental playout until last curtain call)

Printed in England by WEST CENTRAL PRINTING CO. LTD., London and Suffolk